CONTENTS

THE KEY TO 5D

A Guide To Spiritual Awakening

Level 1- Personal Ascension

I dedicate this book to my wonderful partner, Francesca. Without her love, support, kindness and patience, this course could not have been created. Thank you, my love.

INTRODUCTION

Welcome fellow being of love and light to this spiritual awakening course. I want to first thank you for purchasing this book. Something has sparked within you that has triggered your search for something more in life, and I am honoured you have followed your inner guidance which has urged you to buy this book. I wrote this book because I have been on a long awakening journey myself, and I always felt like it would have been a much shorter and easier journey had there been a book like this which guided me through my awakening. Many people do not know where to start on their spiritual journey, so it is my hope that this book offers you the good starting point and foundation that you are looking for.

Before my spiritual awakening, I had what you may call a fairly normal average life. However, I was always rebellious, not just accepting what I was told. In fact, I left one of my jobs because my manager was frustrated that I wouldn't just blindly obey them without asking for justification. My parents and teachers all had the same frustration with me, but it has been my nature to always ask 'why?'. This may have made me a nightmare son, employee and student, but this questioning attitude was vital in helping me spiritually awaken. I always felt there was something more to life, but I didn't know what. I grew up in a very orthodox Christian family, but

Christianity didn't feel quite right for me. I felt there was still something missing. While I didn't have many external troubles, my suffering was all in my mind. I always had emotions and thoughts of anger, fear, guilt, anxiety, boredom, loneliness, and unworthiness. While I was a decent person, I just didn't like people that much because I thought most people were just mean and selfish. I didn't trust anyone, and I didn't feel like there was much joy in life.

My spiritual awakening then began in the summer of 2018. I had an inner urge to stop drinking alcohol while at the same time being urged to start to meditate. After fighting these urges for a short while, the urges became stronger and stronger until I gave in. I then began to hear the phrase "Everything is an illusion" in my head constantly. I didn't give it much thought at first, but then I eventually did some research to find out what illusions this could be referring to. This began a beautiful journey of discovering the hidden truths of reality. During this journey, I was fortunate to have a lot of time on my hands because I was self-employed. This allowed me to do a lot of research into ancient religions, science, recent spiritual downloads, and other resources that most people would simply not have the time to explore. My biggest strength is being able to pick things up really quickly, and that's because I cannot take anything at face value unless I really understand how it all works. This allowed me to really understand spiritual principles and integrate them into my life. Having so much time on my hands also allowed me to try different spiritual exercises and practices and find out what worked for me. In addition, I had a few psychedelic experiences that confirmed to me what I had learned. I transformed my life and I now live in total peace, love, joy and compassion. Every moment in my life is beautiful. You could say that I am living heaven on earth. During this journey, I have also been trained in several healing practices. It then became apparent to me that I was now to teach what I had learned. What use is all this knowledge and joy if I cannot share it? So I set up my business, 'High Vibe Livin', where I help people through alternative healing and spiritual guidance.

What I found on my journey was that there is a universal truth – this truth is at the root of all religions, all science, and within us all. However, this truth has been kept hidden from us. The aim of this book is to help guide you to rediscover this universal truth within yourself. This truth will allow you to ascend to a higher state of consciousness and experience a much more beautiful reality. A lot of this book is written through my own perspective, and your perspective may turn out to be slightly different from mine, so I encourage you to only take what resonates with you. Please don't feel forced into aligning with all my perspectives but listen to your inner feelings while reading to find out what feels right for you. The exercises after each topic are designed to help you integrate the topics within your daily life. After all, it's one thing to read everything, but it is almost useless if you don't actually feel the journey within you and be the living embodiment of the universal truth. If you like any particular exercises, or if you find any particular ones useful, then please don't feel like you have to stop these exercises when you move through the course. I encourage you to keep doing any exercises that you are benefiting from, in addition to doing the daily exercises prescribed. Ultimately, the aim is to completely integrate these exercises into your daily life.

The book has been designed in a way where the reader is to read one topic a week. In between the topics, the reader is encouraged to do the daily exercises prescribed. In my opinion, this is the best way to do the course. But some of you may think differently to me, so you may prefer to read all the topics first and then start on the daily exercises. However, please don't disregard or ignore the exercises – in a way, they are the most important parts of this course. I have based the exercises on what has helped me and others on our journeys. I ask that you do the topics in order as each topic has been carefully structured to flow nicely from the information from previous topics. I hope you enjoy this wonderful journey. If you ever need more personal guidance or healing then please feel free to book a spiritual support or healing session with me through my website: www.highvibelivin.co.uk. It will be my honour to help you in any way that I can.

TOPIC 1 - WHO ARE YOU?

If you thought that there would be some kind of warm up to this course, you are mistaken. In this week's topic, we are jumping straight into the most important question you could ask yourself: Who are you? Isn't it amazing how much of our lives we go through without ever asking ourselves this question? Who am I? To discover who you are, you must first break down who you are not:

1) Your first response to the question of "Who am I?" might be to say something like, "I'm Jamie, I'm a 32 year-old man, I'm an accountant, I'm a father of 3. I'm British." But are these things you have come to know about yourself through self-enquiry, or are these labels that have been put on you by the outer world? Did you come up with your name or was it given to you? Did you discover that you were 32 years-old or was your age defined by a measurement of time that had nothing to do with you? Did you give yourself your job title or was it given to you by your employer? Did you discover you were British, or was this nationality given to you by the country you live in? What's more, all these labels are just the experiences you are having in your life. These experiences change year-in year-out, so does that mean who you really are

changes all the time? Is there no permanent you? Does your age define you? Does your job define you? Does your name define you? If you were not a parent, does this mean there is no you? If you didn't have all these labels, would you not exist? These are all just experiences. You are experiencing being a British man called Jamie. You are currently experiencing the age of 32. You are experiencing being an accountant. You are experiencing being a parent. Ask yourself "Who is it that is having these experiences?". Similarly, you might define yourself by what you have experienced in the past, such as traumas and challenges. Again, these are just experiences; who is the experiencer?

2) So we have established that you are not defined by your experiences. Next, you might say that you are the physical body that is reading this course. But your body is made out of atoms, and only 0.000001% of atoms is physical matter. So if you believe you are a physical body, you are ignoring 99.9999% of who you are. What's more, near-death experiences tell us that, even when the body and brain physically die, people still have very real experiences with their consciousness. They are able to accurately recall information about objects or people in the same room, or those several miles away, when they were supposedly medically dead. Near-death experiences have been scientifically validated several times. Therefore, the real you is independent of the body.

3) Next, you might perhaps say that you are your mind; that you are the voice in your head. But then does that mean you do not exist in the few moments of the day when there is no voice in your head or when you have no thoughts? And have you always had that voice in your head? Think back to when you were a young child. Of

course not - young children can barely talk, so does that mean you didn't exist when you were a young child and had no voice in your head? And is it really you who is controlling the voice in your head? If you think it is, simply close your eyes and try not to think about anything for two minutes. If you control the voice in your head, you should be able to switch it off for a couple of minutes, right? Cue the "I can quit any time I want. I'm just a social thinker" responses. Go on then, try it now. If you are the voice in your head, who was it that was observing the voice in your head during this exercise? Who is the voice in your head talking to?

4) Some of us define who we are (perhaps not consciously) with our status, belongings, assets, power, and/ or popularity, but this means that you have identified yourself with things outside of you. You have ignored who you are inside and have looked outside of you to define yourself. Does this mean you don't exist without all these things?

And now we are left with the stunned humble silence – who are you if not all these things? Sit with this feeling for a moment. You have never had this feeling before so sit with it for a while.

What if I told you that you were leading a double life? What if I told you that you have a false self and a true self? We have all created a false self, called the ego. The ego is the individual character that we play - it is what we think we are in relation to the world around us. This ego is influenced by the experiences that we have had in our lives, like our upbringing, education, religious influences, social influences from colleagues, friends and society, cultural influences, and the media that we consume.

As part of its character, the ego associates itself with the physical body and mind, and it thinks it is separate from everyone else. The ego is a program in your mind that is based on illusory beliefs of separation, and it is the ego program in your mind that generates the voice in your head. As we will discover during this course, it is our association with our ego that creates all our suffering.

The character you play changes year-in year-out based on the different experiences you have. But what is true can never change. When someone tells you the truth about something, the story is always the same. When someone tells you a lie about something, the story changes each time you ask them about it. Only falseness can change, and only truth can be permanent. Scientific concepts, if true, will always stand the test of time. Those concepts and theories that are false disintegrate over time, like the flat earth theory. What is true is permanent, and what is false changes or eventually dies. So the ever-changing character you play cannot be your true self. Similarly, the physical body cannot be your true self because it ages, fluctuates between sickness and health, and eventually dies.

Think about the times when you have committed acts that you regret. Why did you do those things if later you realised that you shouldn't have? It is because the ego program within your subconscious mind took over in those moments and impulsively reacted without your conscious control. Then, after calming down and allowing yourself to think rationally, you realised that your reaction was wrong. That's why you may tell people afterwards "I wasn't thinking straight" or "It was an impulse reaction", or "I couldn't control myself" or "I didn't realise what I was doing". We only regret actions that we believe do not reflect who we truly are. Would you regret showing someone some love? Why not? Because it feels right, it feels good, it feels like we have done something that reflects who we truly are.

After hearing this, you might think, "The ego sounds like a terrible being, why do we associate ourselves with it?". Well, this is what we have been brought up and taught to believe is who we are, and it is what everyone around us thinks they are. We have created such busy lives for ourselves (both in the physical world and in our minds) that do not allow us the time, energy, or motivation to explore who we truly are. But luckily, I'm here to tell you that this false self is simply an illusion you have created; a nightmare you are dreaming. Your true self is waiting quietly to be discovered, and when you do discover it, your life will transform in a magnificent way.

So who really are you? What is your true self? No one can tell you who you really are; it must be experienced for yourself. This is because of two main reasons: 1) If I was to use words to explain who you are, your mind would just use this as another label, which would stop you finding out for yourself who you are. It would become another borrowed belief rather than your truth of who you are. Words are for your mind, and you must go beyond your mind to find out who you are, so words are useless. 2) Who you are cannot be explained by words; words do not do you justice. How do you define stillness? The absence of movement, but do these words do stillness justice? How do you define silence? The absence of noise, but these words are not enough. How do you define nothingness? The absence of something. How do you define emptiness? The absence of something. Similarly, how can I describe who you are? By saying it is the absence of all these labels you used to believe define you. But these words will not do you justice. You have to experience for yourself what stillness, silence, nothingness and emptiness are in order to know them, and you must experience who you are for yourself to really know. I cannot tell you who you are, but I can point to who you are. If you ask me "What is the moon?", and I tell you about it in words, you will have heard about it but you will not have known the moon for yourself. However, if I point to the moon, you can look to where I'm pointing and see it for yourself. The best thing I can do is to help you identify all the disguises you have put on yourself, help you see the falseness of these disguises, help you take these disguises off, and point to what is beyond these disguises. It's then up to you to look where I'm pointing.

Think about it - isn't there a part of you that has always been the same? This part of you is who you truly are. It has never changed and will never change. The ever-changing layers of disguise you have put on yourself, known as your ego, are just on the surface. Go beyond the surface to your very core being, and you will remember that you are the observer rather than the observed, the experiencer rather than the experience. The real you has been called many names: consciousness, awareness, love, oneness, God, etc, but as I mentioned before, these words do not do you justice. Our bodies age and our minds develop, but this awareness stays exactly the same at all times. We all experience this pure awareness, unclouded by the false self, just before we fall asleep every night, and the few seconds just after we wake up every morning. At these times, we feel no sense of individual self. Whenever you have just woken up, there are a few seconds where you don't know who you are or where you are. You do not feel like an individual character during those seconds; you are just pure awareness. This awareness is not bound by the illusory confines of an individual character or body. With meditation, you will realise that your awareness/consciousness is everything and everywhere, and it is permanent. You are all there is, ever was, and ever will be. Any form of individuality is nothing but an illusion. Your false self, your ego, is just a dream. But you are not the dream; you are the dreamer. And, just like a bad nightmare, you will feel an immediate sense of relief once you wake up and realise your true self and true reality. My beloved friend, awakening from the nightmare of separation and discovering your true self is the whole purpose of your spiritual journey here on Earth. Nothing can be more rewarding. All that is needed to remember who you truly are is a sincere inner longing to remember, meditation, and a little patience. Hopefully, with the guidance of this course, the journey to remembering will be shorter. Start with the exercises below which will guide you to discover more about your true self.

Topic 1 Exercises

Day 1

For 10 minutes today, close your eyes and simply notice the thoughts that pop up in your head. Notice how these thoughts arise without your conscious control. Notice what these thoughts are about. Notice how these thoughts make you feel.

Day 2

Today, just take 15 minutes out of your day to look at the sky. I want you to look beyond the clouds to the clear blue sky as much as possible during these 15 minutes. Don't get distracted by the clouds. Try to find the boundary where this blue sky ends. The blue sky represents your awareness, and the clouds represent your thoughts. If you have too many clouds or you get distracted by clouds easily, you will be unable to see the blue sky. Similarly, if you have too many thoughts in your mind or get easily distracted by thoughts, you will be unable to see your awareness. Just as the blue sky has no boundary, so too does your awareness not have any boundaries or limits.

Day 3

For 10 minutes today, close your eyes and ask yourself "Who am I?", and then wait in anticipation. Wait for the answer to come to you. Is the 'you' who asked the question the same as the 'you' who is waiting silently?

Day 4

During the day, repeat the affirmation "I am all there is, ever was, and ever will be". Whenever you can, just say this phrase in your head or out loud. How do you feel as you say it? Is there a part of you that feels that this affirmation is true? And is there another part of you that is resisting saying this affirmation? Why do you think this part of you is resisting?

Day 5

Today, just before you take your shower, I'd like you to visualise each label or experience you used to think defined you as a layer of disguise on your body. Then, as you take your shower, visualise and feel that these layers of disguise are all dissolving and running down the drain. Do not end the shower until all the layers of disguise have dissolved away. As you dry yourself after the shower, notice how much lighter and free you feel after cleansing away the dense disguises that were constricting you and weighing you down.

Day 6

Whenever you are doing anything today, realise that the activity you are doing is just an experience that your awareness is having. Your awareness observes in stillness and silence while your body moves and your mouth talks. So, when you are running or walking, notice how your awareness is still and silent while your body is moving and passing your surroundings. As you cook, notice how your awareness is observing the whole process. Who you truly are is the observer of everything you do and everything that happens to you. In this way, you are taking a backseat and watching your day as if it was a film on a screen. Alternatively, you can view it as your awareness being immersed in a virtual reality game – everything around you looks real and looks like it is moving, but your awareness is in one spot the whole time.

Day 7

Today, I would like you to go on to the 'High Vibe Livin' Youtube channel and play the video called 'Guided Meditation to Discover Your True Self'. This video will guide you through the meditation. I hope you enjoy it.

TOPIC 2 - ONENESS

As discussed in the previous topic, your ego is a set of false beliefs about who you are in relation to the world around you. This individual character believes it is separate from everything and everyone. But we have established that your ego is nothing but a figment of your imagination. Who you truly are is awareness, and this awareness has no boundaries. It is what permeates all things in the universe. It is all that exists. Without the illusory boundaries created by your mind that separates all things, you would be able to recognise that, in fact, there is no separation. There is only you. There is only oneness.

Oneness is not a new concept - many religions, spiritual societies, scientists and philosophers have tried to tell us that everything in the universe is connected and that there is no separation at all. But this universal truth has been consistently dismissed, suppressed and kept hidden throughout human history. Let's look at what some of them have said about oneness:

Neoplatonism, named after the Greek philosopher Plato, proposed the existence of deep interconnections among all things, including what is normally viewed as the distinction between mental and physical phenomena. From the everyday, ego-based state of awareness, mind and matter appear to be fundamentally different. But from the state of gnosis, which provides direct access to higher states of existence, the apparent distinctions between mind and matter, or space and time, are revealed as illusions. From our individual awareness, we see objects separated in space and time, and we see obvious differences between mental and physical phenomena. But from a higher state of consciousness, all such differences dissolve, and naked reality is experienced as entangled relationships in a holistic reality, completely free of the constraints of space or time. From a higher state of consciousness, you can directly perceive what the lower state of consciousness experiences as the future or the past, and you also transcend the distinctions that separate you from other objects.

Hermetic Cosmology (named after Hermes, the son of Greek god Zeus) contends that reality consists of a single Universal Consciousness. In Hermeticism, this single Universal Consciousness appears in two complementary aspects, like the two sides of the same coin. One form is a manifested, primordial, "plastic" energy, known as the One Thing. The other form is a non-manifested, transcendent element known as the One Mind. The One Thing reacts to and is shaped by the One Mind. The One Mind only has the appearance of being different from the One Thing. Similarly, personal consciousness is not separate from the physical world.

Two thousand years ago, the father of modern medicine, Hippocrates, observed, "There is one common flow, one common breathing, all things are in sympathy. The whole organism and each one of its parts are working in conjunction for the same purpose... The great principle extends to the extremist part, and from the extremist part it returns to the great principle, to the one nature, being and not being".

Roman emperor and philosopher Marcus Aurelius believed, "Everything is connected and the web is holy".

Albert Einstein said: "A human being is a part of the whole, called by us 'Universe', a part limited in time and space. He experiences himself, his thoughts and feeling as something separated from the rest – a kind of optical delusion of his consciousness". When we begin to "free ourselves from this prison", as Einstein phrased it, we can then expand our consciousness to "embrace all living creatures and the whole of nature." Our consciousness interacts with the energy of the universe.

Indian Vedic philosophy holds that the great nonlocal universal consciousness is reflected in each of us. The analogy is that of buckets of water in which the sun is reflected. Though there are many different buckets, it is the same sun reflecting in all of them.

The most important characteristic of the Eastern world view – one could almost say the essence of it – is the awareness of the unity and mutual interrelation of all things and events; the experience of all phenomena in the world as manifestations of basic oneness. All things are seen as interdependent and inseparable parts of the cosmic whole; as different manifestations of the same ultimate reality. The Eastern traditions constantly refer to this ultimate, indivisible reality which manifests itself in all things, and of which all things are parts. It is called Brahman in Hinduism, Dharmakaya in Buddhism, and Tao in Taoism.

In Christianity, the Bible does reference the oneness of all things several times. For example, in the book of Corinthians, it says, "For by one Spirit are we all baptized into one body, whether we be Jews or Gentiles, whether we be bond or free; and have been all made to drink into one Spirit.". It is saying that there is one spirit that manifests into different bodies. In the book of Ephesians, it says "One God and Father of all, who is above all, and through all, and in you all." It is saying that there is an entity, called here "God", within everything and everyone.

Sufism, a branch of Islam, recognises one central truth, it is the unity of being, that we are not separate from the Divine. We are One: one people, one ecology, one universe, one being. If there is a single truth, worthy of the name, it is that we are all integral to the Truth, not separate. They believe that the essence of being, also termed as Truth or God, is devoid of every form and quality, and hence unmanifested, yet it is inseparable from every form and phenomenon, either material or spiritual.

Gnosticism is a religion based on sacred knowledge obtained only through the state of gnosis, where a higher state of consciousness is achieved through meditation or psychedelics. They believe that all is God, for all consists of the substance of God. The gospel of Thomas, for example, focuses on oneness, seeing through the duality of the mainstream Jewish religion of the day.

Taoism is an Eastern philosophy that is based completely on oneness, which is referred to as 'Tao'. As the founder of Taoism, Lao Tzu, once said, "Filled with infinite possibilities and one with the dust, the Tao unites the world into one whole like a deep pool that never dries up."

How you treat others a reflection of how you are treating yourself

ANDREW NAROUZ

Within the esoteric worldview, there is no outside world, no separation, no time. Everything is already within consciousness, which is beyond ordinary space-time. Said another way, when the Indian sage Ramana Maharshi was asked, "How are we to treat others?", his reply was simple: "There are no others".

Many of those who have had near-death experiences or psychedelic experiences often report a sense of oneness and a sudden understanding that everything is connected.

The Field

So, what are all these people talking about? Where is the evidence for this oneness and the interconnections of the Universe? We certainly can't see or feel these connections, right? Most of us perceive our reality based on what our body's five senses allow us to perceive. Usually, something only exists to us if we can see, smell, taste, hear or touch it. This is because many of us believe we are our body, as was discussed in the last topic. By solely relying on the body's senses, we perceive that we are separate from others, from things, from life, from God. The mind makes us believe that there is a past and future, and that there is space separating things in the universe. We believe life just happens to us, independent of our control. But what if our senses deceive us? What if our bodies were designed to view an illusory experience? What if, like virtual reality, our bodies are perceiving something different to what is truly there? Just because we can't sense something, it doesn't mean that it doesn't exist – can you feel or see gravity? Or magnetic fields? Or Wi-Fi? I remember in school when we thought we were so funny by playing a high frequency tone from our phones that only those aged below 30 could hear, so the teachers never heard it – just because they couldn't hear it, it doesn't mean that the tone wasn't there.

As we have established, religions and philosophers have talked about an interlinking interdependent oneness of the universe, but what is the scientific evidence of this oneness? We have been taught that the basic building blocks of everything in the universe are atoms, and that atoms are made up of a nucleus with surrounding electrons. However, quantum physicists found that 99.99999999% of an atom appears to be empty space. But this space isn't really empty; it's made up of a vast array of energetic frequencies that make up an invisible, interconnected field of information. In physics, this single field of information is called the unified field or zero point field or aetheric field. Like fishes in the sea, the pressure of this energetic "fluid" constantly surrounds us, though we do not normally notice its presence. If you were to ask fish what it is like swimming in water, they would ask you "what's water?". We don't realise that we are moving through the aetheric field, just like fish don't realise they are in water. As will be explained later in this topic, the aether is a source of tremendous energy that is in constant vibrational motion, flowing through all objects in the universe, creating and recreating them every second. Should this aether ever stop flowing and swirling about with such an intelligent, purposeful behaviour, all mass would shed heat, gradually dissolve, and return to its primordial energy state.

Even what we thought we knew as the physical parts of the atom, the nucleus and electrons, which make up 0.000000001% of the atom, quantum theory has now proven that these particles simply dissolve into wave-like patterns of probabilities, and that these patterns, ultimately, do not represent probabilities of physical things, but rather probabilities of interconnections. This new physics of the 21st century tells us that the very building blocks of mass, molecules and the atoms themselves, are not particles at all. Instead, they are ultimately nothing more than spherical whirlpools of energy in this flowing river of aether. With this matrix, all elements of the cosmos are very intimately and directly connected through "synchronicity", as defined by Dr Carl Jung, who said that every event in a particular space and time is fundamentally connected to every other event in that space and time.

We therefore live in a harmonic universe, built upon a unified, unseen foundation of conscious, loving energy, known as "zero point energy" or "aether." This invisible energy field is the One Divine Consciousness that organises all of creation and is within all of creation. Could this field of energy be what the book of Acts in the Bible means when it says: "God...is not far from any one of us. For in him we live and move and have our being"? Similarly, the Universe is thought of as one by the small number of aborigines who survive. Aboriginal cultures do not make the usual distinctions among rocks, air and humans. All are imbued with spirit, the invisible energy. This invisible energy is describing the zero point energy.

Scientists recently mapped out this cosmic web, and it looks like the neural pathways in the brain. That is such a powerful analogy in itself, where the universe is one single brain, and the different beings, planets, stars and galaxies are simply different neurons all connected to each other within this brain.

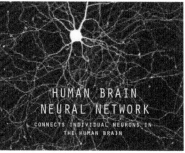

Field Energy

So what is the proof that this zero point energy field exists? How do we know it isn't in fact just empty space? Well, if these areas of the universe are truly empty, then nothing should be there; no electromagnetic fields, no X-rays, no heat, no energy, nothing. In order to test this idea in the laboratory, it was necessary to create an area that was completely free of air (a vacuum) and shield it from all known electromagnetic radiation fields. The shielding of this "empty" area from energy fields was accomplished by using what is known as a Faraday cage, which is lined with lead. This airless vacuum was then cooled down to absolute zero – the temperature where all matter should stop vibrating and thus produce no heat. At this point, all conventional explanations would simply say that it should be a dead, lifeless "vacuum". Then, inside that area, two perfectly flat metallic plates were moved very, very close to each other. What do you think would happen? We are quick to conclude that this simple experiment shouldn't do anything. However, under these circumstances, when the two plates are moved together, they experience a terrific attraction that seems to pull them together with a tremendous amount of force. This is because when two plates are placed near each other, the zero-point waves between the plates are restricted to those that essentially span the gap. Since some wavelengths of the field are excluded, this leads to a disturbance in the equilibrium of the field and the result is an imbalance of energy, with less energy in the gap between the plates than in the outside empty space. This greater energy density pushes the two metal plates together. This is what is known as the "Casimir Force," named after the man who discovered it, Dutch physicist Hendrick Casimir. This experimental effect also revealed that if you actually allow the two plates to completely merge, the force that binds them together is so powerful that you literally have to destroy them to get them back apart. Now think about that for a minute; how would one explain a force that could "suck" two plates together so strongly?

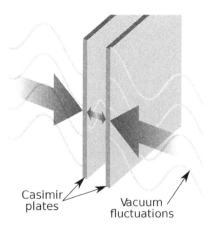

Casimir plates

Vacuum fluctuations

Constant Interactions with the Field

As discussed in the previous topic, your ego is a set of false beliefs about who you are in relation to the world around you. This individual character believes it is separate from everything and everyone. But we have established that your ego is nothing but a figment of your imagination. Who you truly are is awareness, and this awareness has no boundaries. It is what permeates all things in the universe. It is all that exists. Without the illusory boundaries created by your mind that separates all things, you would be able to recognise that, in fact, there is no separation. There is only you. There is only oneness.

Oneness is not a new concept - many religions, spiritual societies, scientists and philosophers have tried to tell us that everything in the universe is connected and that there is no separation at all. But this universal truth has been consistently dismissed, suppressed and kept hidden throughout human history. Let's look at what some of them have said about oneness:

Neoplatonism, named after the Greek philosopher Plato, proposed the existence of deep interconnections among all things, including what is normally viewed as the distinction between mental and physical phenomena. From the everyday, ego-based state of awareness, mind and matter appear to be fundamentally different. But from the state of gnosis, which provides direct access to higher states of existence, the apparent distinctions between mind and matter, or space and time, are revealed as illusions. From our individual awareness, we see objects separated in space and time, and we see obvious differences between mental and physical phenomena. But from a higher state of consciousness, all such differences dissolve, and naked reality is experienced as entangled relationships in a holistic reality, completely free of the constraints of space or time. From a higher state of consciousness, you can directly perceive what the lower state of consciousness experiences as the future or the past, and you also transcend the distinctions that separate you from other objects.

Hermetic Cosmology (named after Hermes, the son of Greek god Zeus) contends that reality consists of a single Universal Consciousness. In Hermeticism, this single Universal Consciousness appears in two complementary aspects, like the two sides of the same coin. One form is a manifested, primordial, "plastic" energy, known as the One Thing. The other form is a non-manifested, transcendent element known as the One Mind. The One Thing reacts to and is shaped by the One Mind. The One Mind only has the appearance of being different from the One Thing. Similarly, personal consciousness is not separate from the physical world.

Two thousand years ago, the father of modern medicine, Hippocrates, observed, "There is one common flow, one common breathing, all things are in sympathy. The whole organism and each one of its parts are working in conjunction for the same purpose... The great principle extends to the extremist part, and from the extremist part it returns to the great principle, to the one nature, being and not being".

Roman emperor and philosopher Marcus Aurelius believed, "Everything is connected and the web is holy".

Albert Einstein said: "A human being is a part of the whole, called by us 'Universe', a part limited in time and space. He experiences himself, his thoughts and feeling as something separated from the rest – a kind of optical delusion of his consciousness". When we begin to "free ourselves from this prison", as Einstein phrased it, we can then expand our consciousness to "embrace all living creatures and the whole of nature." Our consciousness interacts with the energy of the universe.

Indian Vedic philosophy holds that the great nonlocal universal consciousness is reflected in each of us. The analogy is that of buckets of water in which the sun is reflected. Though there are many different buckets, it is the same sun reflecting in all of them.

The most important characteristic of the Eastern world view – one could almost say the essence of it – is the awareness of the unity and mutual interrelation of all things and events; the experience of all phenomena in the world as manifestations of basic oneness. All things are seen as interdependent and inseparable parts of the cosmic whole; as different manifestations of the same ultimate reality. The Eastern traditions constantly refer to this ultimate, indivisible reality which manifests itself in all things, and of which all things are parts. It is called Brahman in Hinduism, Dharmakaya in Buddhism, and Tao in Taoism. Taoism is an Eastern philosophy that is based completely on oneness, which is referred to as 'Tao'. As the founder of Taoism, Lao Tzu, once said, "Filled with infinite possibilities and one with the dust, the Tao unites the world into one whole like a deep pool that never dries up."

In Christianity, the Bible does reference the oneness of all things several times. For example, in the book of Corinthians, it says, "For by one Spirit are we all baptized into one body, whether we be Jews or Gentiles, whether we be bond or free; and have been all made to drink into one Spirit.". It is saying that there is one spirit that manifests into different bodies. In the book of Ephesians, it says "One God and

Father of all, who is above all, and through all, and in you all." It is saying that there is an entity, called here "God", within everything and everyone.

Sufism, a branch of Islam, recognises one central truth, it is the unity of being, that we are not separate from the Divine. We are One: one people, one ecology, one universe, one being. If there is a single truth, worthy of the name, it is that we are all integral to the Truth, not separate. They believe that the essence of being, also termed as Truth or God, is devoid of every form and quality, and hence unmanifested, yet it is inseparable from every form and phenomenon, either material or spiritual.

Gnosticism is a religion based on sacred knowledge obtained only through the state of gnosis, where a higher state of consciousness is achieved through meditation or psychedelics. They believe that all is God, for all consists of the substance of God. The gospel of Thomas, for example, focuses on oneness, seeing through the duality of the mainstream Jewish religion of the day.

Within the esoteric worldview, there is no outside world, no separation, no time. Everything is already within consciousness, which is beyond ordinary space-time. Said another way, when the Indian sage Ramana Maharshi was asked, "How are we to treat others?", his reply was simple: "There are no others".

Many of those who have had near-death experiences or psychedelic experiences often report a sense of oneness and a sudden understanding that everything is connected.

The Field

So, what are all these people talking about? Where is

the evidence for this oneness and the interconnections of the Universe? We certainly can't see or feel these connections, right? Most of us perceive our reality based on what our body's five senses allow us to perceive. Usually, something only exists to us if we can see, smell, taste, hear or touch it. This is because many of us believe we are our body, as was discussed in the last topic. By solely relying on the body's senses, we perceive that we are separate from others, from things, from life, from God. The mind makes us believe that there is a past and future, and that there is space separating things in the universe. We believe life just happens to us, independent of our control. But what if our senses deceive us? What if our bodies were designed to view an illusory experience? What if, like virtual reality, our bodies are perceiving something different to what is truly there? Just because we can't sense something, it doesn't mean that it doesn't exist – can you feel or see gravity? Or magnetic fields? Or Wi-Fi? I remember in school when we thought we were so funny by playing a high frequency tone from our phones that only those aged below 30 could hear, so the teachers never heard it – just because they couldn't hear it, it doesn't mean that the tone wasn't there.

As we have established, religions and philosophers have talked about an interlinking interdependent oneness of the universe, but what is the scientific evidence of this oneness? We have been taught that the basic building blocks of everything in the universe are atoms, and that atoms are made up of a nucleus with surrounding electrons. However, quantum physicists found that 99.99999999% of an atom appears to be empty space. But this space isn't really empty; it's made up of a vast array of energetic frequencies that make up an invisible, interconnected field of information. In physics, this single field of information is called the unified field or zero point field or aetheric field. Like fishes in the sea, the pressure of this energetic "fluid" constantly surrounds us, though we do not normally notice its presence. If you were to ask fish what it is like swimming in water, they would ask you "what's water?". We don't realise that we are moving through the aetheric field, just like fish don't realise they are in water. As will be explained later in this topic, the aether is a source of tremendous energy that is in constant vibrational motion, flowing through all objects in the universe, creating and recreating them every second. Should this aether ever stop flowing and swirling about with such an intelligent, purposeful behaviour, all mass would shed heat, gradually dissolve, and return to its primordial energy state.

Even what we thought we knew as the physical parts of the atom, the nucleus and electrons, which make up 0.000000001% of the atom, quantum theory has now proven that these particles simply dissolve into wave-like patterns of probabilities, and that these patterns, ultimately, do not represent probabilities of physical things, but rather probabilities of interconnections. This new physics of the 21st century tells us that the very building blocks of mass, molecules and the atoms themselves, are not particles at all. Instead, they are ultimately nothing more than spherical whirlpools of energy in this flowing river of aether. With this matrix, all elements of the cosmos are very intimately and directly connected through "synchronicity", as defined by Dr Carl Jung, who said that every event in a particular space and time is fundamentally connected to every other event in that space and time.

We therefore live in a harmonic universe, built upon a unified, unseen foundation of conscious, loving energy, known as "zero point energy" or "aether." This invisible energy field is the One Divine Consciousness that organises all of creation and is within all of creation. Could this field of energy be what the book of Acts in the Bible means when it says: "God...is not far from any one of us. For in him we live and move and have our being"? Similarly, the Universe is thought of as one by the small number of aborigines who survive. Aboriginal cultures do not make the usual distinctions among rocks, air and humans. All are imbued with spirit, the invisible energy. This invisible energy is describing the zero point energy.

Scientists recently mapped out this cosmic web, and it looks like the neural pathways in the brain. That is such a powerful analogy in itself, where the universe is one single brain, and the different beings, planets, stars and galaxies are simply different neurons all connected to each other within this brain.

Field Energy

So what is the proof that this zero point energy field exists? How do we know it isn't in fact just empty space? Well, if these areas of the universe are truly empty, then nothing should be there; no electromagnetic fields, no X-rays, no heat, no energy, nothing. In order to test this idea in the laboratory, it was necessary to create an area that was completely free of air (a vacuum) and shield it from all known electromagnetic radiation fields. The shielding of this "empty" area from energy fields was accomplished by using what is known as a Faraday cage, which is lined with lead. This airless vacuum was then cooled down to absolute zero – the temperature where all matter should stop vibrating and thus produce no heat. At this point, all conventional explanations would simply say that it should be a dead, lifeless "vacuum". Then, inside that area, two perfectly flat metallic plates were moved very, very close to each other. What do you think would happen? We are quick to conclude that this simple experiment shouldn't do anything. However, under these circumstances, when the two plates are moved together, they experience a terrific attraction that seems to pull them together with a tremendous amount of force. This is because when two plates are placed near each other, the zero-point waves between the plates are restricted to those that essentially span the gap. Since some wavelengths of the field are excluded, this leads to a disturbance in the equilibrium of the field and the result is an imbalance of energy, with less energy in the gap between the plates than in the outside empty space. This greater energy density pushes the two metal plates together. This is what is known as the "Casimir Force," named after the man who discovered it, Dutch physicist Hendrick Casimir. This experimental effect also revealed that if you actually allow the two plates to completely merge, the force that binds them together is so powerful that you literally have to destroy them to get them back apart. Now think about that for a minute; how would one explain a force that could "suck" two plates together so strongly?

Constant Interactions with the Field

Quantum scientists struggled with the question of why an electron orbits around a proton, like a planet orbiting around a sun. In the solar system, gravity accounts for the stable orbit. But in the atomic world, any moving electron, which carries a charge, wouldn't be stable like an orbiting planet, but would eventually radiate away, or exhaust its energy and then spiral into the nucleus, causing the entire atomic structure of the object to collapse, as a satellite will eventually do in Earth orbit. But Timothy Boyer and Dr Hal Puthoff showed mathematically that, if you take into account the zero point field, electrons lose and gain energy constantly from this field in a dynamic equilibrium, balanced exactly at the right orbit. Electrons get their energy to keep going without slowing down because they are refuelling by tapping into these fluctuations of empty space. In other words, the zero point field accounts for the stability of all matter. So, all objects in our universe, regardless of their size, are consistently drawing in aetheric energy to sustain their existence. Without this ongoing influx of energy to support themselves, they would shed heat and dissolve back into aether. Hal also showed by physics calculations that fluctuations of the zero point field waves drive the motion of subatomic particles, and that all the motion of all the particles in the universe in turn generates the zero point field - a sort of self-generating feedback loop across the cosmos. This means that we, and all matter in the universe, are engaged in a constant two-way interaction with the aetheric field.

Spontaneous emission, where atoms decay and emit radiation for no known reason has also been shown to be a zero point field effect. These experiments have demonstrated that the very reason for the universe's stability is an exchange of energy between all "matter" and the zero point field.

The Mystery of Inertia

Newton composed a series of laws including the "law of

inertia," which can be explained simply as: "An object at rest tends to stay at rest, and an object in motion tends to stay in motion." And that means that, even in an airless vacuum without gravity, you will encounter a force that will cause you to have difficulty moving something through space. The million-dollar question is why? Bernie, Rueda and Puthoff published a paper in a very prestigious physical journal that demonstrated that the property of inertia possessed by all objects in the physical universe was simply resistance to being accelerated through the zero point field. Therefore, this shows us that no matter where we go in the universe, we are always moving through the energy "body" of the zero point field.

Using the Zero Point Field in Today's Technology

Ordinarily, electrons repel each other and don't like to be pushed too closely together. However, you can tightly cluster electronic charge if you calculate in the zero point field, which at some point will begin to push electrons together. This enables you to develop electronic applications in very tiny spaces. Hal and Ken began coming up with gadget applications that would use this energy and then patenting their discoveries. Eventually, they invented a special device that could fit an X-ray device at the end of a hypodermic needle, enabling medics to take pictures of body parts in tiny crevices. They also invented a high frequency signal generator radar device that would allow a radar to be generated from a source no larger than a plastic credit card. In addition, they were among the first to design a flat-panel television with the width of a hanging picture. All their patents were accepted with the explanation that the ultimate source of energy appears to be the zero point radiation of the vacuum continuum.

Bringing All Forces Together

Ultimately, all of the fundamental fields – gravity, electromagnetism, weak nuclear and strong nuclear forces – must emanate directly from the aether, a unifying force of sympathetic vibrations that forms all of physical reality as we now see it. Puthoff demonstrated mathematically how the zero point field brought all these forces of physics into one unified theory.

Time and Space

French physicist Alan Aspect performed a famous quantum physics experiment in the early 1980s called the Bell test experiment. In the study, scientists entangled two photons, causing them to bond together. They then shot the two photons in opposite directions, creating a distance and space between them. When they influenced one photon to disappear, the other photon vanished at exactly the same time. What this showed was that there is a unifying field of information existing beyond three-dimensional space and time that connects all matter. If the two particles of light were not connected by some invisible field of energy, it would have taken time for information to travel from one local point in space to the other local point in space. According to Einstein's theory, if one particle disappeared, the other particle should disappear a moment later, unless they were occupying the same space at the same time. Even if the second photon was affected a millisecond later, because they were separated by space, time would have played a factor in relaying the information. This would have reaffirmed that the ceiling of this physical reality is the speed of light and everything material that exists here is separate. Because the two particles vanished at exactly the same time, it proved that all matter – bodies, objects, places – and even time are connected by frequency and information in a realm beyond three-dimensional reality and time.

Time and space are ultimately related – we perceive a space between two things because it would take time to move from one thing to the other. We all remember the basic science equation: Time = Distance / Speed. In the 'normal' world of material objects, it takes time to move from one space to another. But, as we have learned, 99.99999% of the universe is not material, and is, in fact, composed of the invisible zero point field. When we shift our focus away from the 3D material world of time and space to the invisible world of oneness, time and space disappear.

According to the big bang theory, everything in the universe was once connected, or entangled, into a single, small, dense point of energy. So, just like the entangled photons in the Bell test experiment, this means that everything in the universe is always connected through the cosmic web – where everything affects everything.

Organisms Communicating Through the Field

Cleve Backster conducted an experiment where he burned the leaf of a plant and then measured its galvanic response, much as he would register the skin response of a person being tested for lying. Interestingly enough, the plant registered the same increased-stress polygraph response as a human would if his hand had been burned. Even more fascinating was that Backster had burned the leaf of a neighbouring plant not connected to the equipment. The original plant, still hooked up to the polygraph, again registered the pain response that it had when its own leaves had been burned. This suggested that the first plant had received this information via some extrasensory mechanism and was demonstrating empathy. It seemed to point to some sort of interconnectedness between living things.

The 'Backster effect' had also been seen between plants and animals. When brine shrimp in one location died suddenly, this seemed to instantly register with plants in another location, as recorded on a standard psychogalvanic response instrument. Backster had carried out this type of experiment over several hundred miles, and in each instance, some mysterious communication occurred between living things and plants.

During a talk, Backster revealed that he discovered that when he poured a pot of boiling water from the coffeemaker into the sink in his laboratory, his plants, which were always connected to the polygraph machine, registered a huge and immediate shock. He was very puzzled as to what had caused this at first, and he had to think carefully about what he was doing right at the moment that the shock had registered. Once he traced it back to the boiling water, he sampled the sink with a cotton swab and analysed the specimen under a microscope. He then got the answer, which was that a huge colony of bacteria was growing in the sink, which he did not clean regularly. Subsequent experiments proved that the plants consistently reacted to the death of the bacteria.

Backster conducted other experiments where he removed cheek cells from a participant and stored them in a different room. Tailor-made emotional shocks were then carefully induced to the participant. What he found was that the cheek cells would demonstrate sudden responses that corresponded precisely with the timing of the emotional shocks induced to the participant. It wasn't necessarily easy to ethically shock a human being, so there was no "standardised" way to run the experiment. The tailored shocks were administered through such methods as the viewing of a violent movie footage that would have a particular emotional impact to that individual, such as a World War Two fighter pilot veteran watching a film of an airplane being shot down. In such a case, as the ex-pilot squirmed in his chair, creating electromagnetic frequency changes in his Galvanic Skin Response, his cheek cells would squirm in the next room in the same measurable way. Another example was leaving a young man in a room with a pornographic magazine, and then barging into the room after he had started looking at it, creating a rush of embarrassment. His cells showed the same response in the next room. Therefore, shocks and negative emotions in the mind are instantaneously moving throughout the cells of the body and affecting them, whether those cells are connected to the body or not. If space has no medium in it that allows instantaneous communication between two things, then how could all this be possible?

Superhuman Abilities

Many humans have been noted as having extraordinary abilities, such as psychokinesis (moving matter with your mind), precognition (seeing into the future), remote viewing (where a person can see within their minds a particular target that is inaccessible to normal senses due to distance or time), and levitation. While I will not go into too much detail on this interesting topic, it is important to consider it here.

Ingo Swann had been hired by the CIA to use his remote viewing abilities to help with secret defence operations for the USA. He was once asked to remote view Jupiter just before the upcoming NASA Pioneer 10 flyby launch. During the experiment, Swann was embarrassed to admit that he'd seen and drawn a ring around Jupiter. Perhaps, he told Puthoff, he'd just mistakenly directed his attention toward Saturn. No one was prepared to take the drawing seriously, until the NASA mission revealed that Jupiter indeed had a ring at the time. Swann's experiment demonstrated that humans could, in effect, see or gain access to information at virtually any distance. The SRI remote viewing programme carried on for 23 years behind a wall of secrecy that is still erected. It had been funded entirely by the government. Many famous and Nobel Prize winning scientists worked in the programme. At the close of the programme in 1995, a review was carried out by a sceptic statistics professor, and she agreed that the statistical results for remote-viewing phenomena were far beyond what could have occurred by chance. It seemed to suggest that, because of our constant dialogue with the zero point field, we are everywhere at once.

Dean Radin has conducted many experiments at the Institute for Noetic Sciences to show that our bodies register responses to events before they actually happen. He showed people random pictures, some were shocking, some beautiful and some were not meant to initiate a response. The experiments showed that the bodies of the participants reacted to the pictures before they were actually shown. Before a person was shown a shocking picture, the person's body was reacting to shock. Before a person was shown a beautiful picture, their body showed physiological signs of responses to beauty. This further proves that we can interact with the aetheric field to gather information irrespective of time. This means that all time is one, there is no past or future, only the eternal now. And if there is no time, then there must also be no distance because distance=speed/time; which means that all separation is just an illusion.

Synchronicity

But you don't necessarily need to have an extraordinary ability to see evidence for this oneness in your life. Have you ever had a dream that foretold of something that was to happen later in your life? Have you ever had the feeling that something bad was going to happen, and then something bad happened soon after? Do you regularly notice that the same number(s) keep popping up in your life? I personally see the numbers 23 and 32 everywhere I look. Have you noticed certain events in your life lining up so perfectly that it could not just be down to coincidence? This is called synchronicity, and it shows how everything is linked in our universe. Swiss psychiatrist Carl Jung defined synchronicity as "a meaningful coincidence of two or more events, where something other than the probability of chance is involved". Einstein once said, "Synchronicity is God's way of remaining anonymous".

Following on from the energetic nature of the Universe, Geesink and Meijer found that the human electromagnetic field "communicates bi-directionally with a global electromagnetic field via wave resonance, and comprises a universal consciousness that experiences the sensations, perceptions, thoughts and emotions of every conscious being in the universe". Connect the dots between all the scientific findings and synchronicity suddenly doesn't seem mysterious at all. Frequencies may function as the resonators that entrain micro and macro events in synchronicity. Though we can't see these frequencies, they permeate both mind and matter. We swim in them as a fish swims in water, unaware of the existence of the fundamental fields that shape consciousness and everything in the material world. The intercommunication between these levels of reality provides a plausible scientific explanation for synchronicity. Multidirectional intercommunication fields link us continuously, even if we are unaware of their existence. That linking is how all the unlikely components of anomalous events are able to assemble into synchronicities.

After 9/11, the official estimate of the death toll almost two weeks later from the New York Police Department was 6,659. However, as the months went by and the story kept unfolding, the numbers kept dropping. The final death toll was 2,753. That's less than half the initial estimate. What explains such a huge disparity between the numbers? According to a careful analysis of the question by USA Today, "Many companies did head counts after the attack...Counts from more than 50 floors indicate the buildings were barely half full". Where were the missing people? There are many reasons why people weren't in the World Trade Centre that morning. Some described having been warned by intuition, dreams or precognition. Others experienced unexpected delays due to crowded trains or family problems. These synchronicities ended up saving their lives.

The Link to God

Many have suggested that the aether itself provides the most tangible, scientific way to define, explain and even engineer the Mind of God. As 'A Course in Miracles' states:

"There is no time, no place, no state where God is absent. There is nothing to be feared. There is no way in which a gap could be conceived of in the Wholeness that is His.".

Einstein once said: "Everyone who is seriously involved in the pursuit of science becomes convinced that some spirit is manifest in the laws of the universe, one that is vastly superior to that of man". Max Planck, a founding father of quantum physics, similarly said: "All matter originates and exists only by virtue of a force which brings the particles of an atom to vibration and holds this most minute solar system of the atom together....We must assume behind this force the existence of a conscious and intelligent Mind. This Mind is the matrix of all matter".

By design, our brains and senses only perceive the material world. If we go by our senses, the majority of an atom appears to be an empty black space of nothingness. But in fact, as the science we have discussed has proved, this space is the zero point energy field that is the true essence behind the whole universe. This zero point energy field is God. Since we have discussed how we are connected to the zero point field of the Universe, we must also be connected to this conscious and intelligent mind.

But why would God create the illusion of separation when everything is one? Well, imagine for a moment that you are God – whole and one. You have the unlimited power to create. Unless you create, there is just awareness, just oneness. This awareness is still, silent, empty and nothing. What is there to do but to create and experience your creations? To create experiences is similar to creating a film - but the problem is that you, God, are the only actor. How can there be a film where you are the only character? You must therefore use different disguises and make-up to portray the illusion of different actors. But these actors must think they are separate from each other in order to have a rich experience. If these characters know that they are the same being, the film would be very different. It would be less dramatic for sure. There have to be people who play the bad guys, the leaders, the good guys, the extras, the teachers, the love interests. If you didn't pretend you were all these different characters, there would be no film, no experience.

Let us consider a different analogy – the video game. You decide to play a video game because you want to experience something, and so you play this game where you play different characters throughout. When a game is really good, you get really into it, losing yourself in it and forgetting who you are while playing. So it is with God; he must forget himself and absorb himself in illusions to have different and unique experiences. Like in acting, the more the actor believes they are the character, the more enriching the experience is. Many of those who have had near-death experiences have come back and told us how they interpreted the universe as God playing with itself in this way. But forgetting the truth can only be temporary until the character inevitably realises the falseness around them – like in the Truman Show where Jim Carey starts to realise that his whole life has just been a film that he has been starring in.

Meditation

While awake and interacting with the world, it can be easy to forget the true nature of reality, which is oneness. This is why meditation is so important during your spiritual journey. Meditation allows you to shut out all sensory input and the voice in your head and just be. It is the best way to remind yourself of oneness. As you sit as awareness during meditation, all past and future dissolve away, and there is just presence, oneness, and pure love. This is the secret that we have all kept from ourselves for centuries - all is one. You are everything and everyone. You are all that exists, has ever existed, and will ever exist. Feel the truth of these words within your being. You are simply playing with illusions in order to have experiences based separation. But it is now time to wake up from your dream. These words are simply an alarm you set for yourself to wake up and remember the true nature of reality. Come home, dear one. Come home.

Topic 2 Exercises

<u>Day 1</u>

The eyes are the window to the soul, and at the soul level we are all the same. In this case, the soul I am talking about is the one consciousness that pervades all life. This one consciousness is peering out of every living being's eyes. It is the same one consciousness that is looking out of everybody's eyes. A good way to see oneness is to stare into the centre of the eyes of a being. So today, whenever interacting with people, or whenever you are with your loved one or pet, look into the centre of their eyes. Notice how you feel when you do this. Take some time to look at your own eyes in the mirror. You are staring at your true essence. Notice how all illusions fall away as you look into someone's eyes.

<u>Day 2</u>

Today, set aside 10 minutes and look around the room.

Then, visualise that there is an invisible field within everything and everyone in the room, like a matrix of sorts. This invisible field is within you as well. Feel it. Feel your connection with your surroundings.

Day 3

Today, we are going to repeat the following affirmation several times during the day: "I am one with everything and everyone". How does this affirmation make you feel? How does this exercise change how you behave and interact with life?

Day 4

Today, as you interact with other people, plants, animals and objects, interact with them as if you are interacting with yourself. Imagine they are all you in another form. Does this change how you interact with them? How do you feel when you believe you are interacting with yourself?

Day 5

Take some time today, perhaps 10 to 15 minutes, and pick up an object. It can be any object, but it would be beneficial if it is an object you like. Now just inspect this object, get to know every nook and cranny. If you get distracted by thoughts, return your attention to the object. Notice how you feel towards the object the more you look at it. You will notice that by not succumbing to your mind's constant attempts to distract you with thoughts based on separation, you can feel closer to an object. You are able to realise how the object is a part of you.

Day 6

Take 10 minutes today to close your eyes and visualise someone you are angry with or don't get along with. Picture them in your mind. Now, imagine that person is just you but in a different body. They are playing a different character but, ultimately, they are the same consciousness as you. How do you feel about them now? Do you still feel anger or hatred towards them? Why has this anger gone, or why has it reduced? What this exercise shows is that by truly perceiving your oneness with someone, it is hard to be angry with them. This is because love and oneness are two sides of the same coin. How can you be angry at yourself? Repeat this exercise with anyone else you feel hatred or anger towards.

Day 7

Today, I would like you to go on to the 'High Vibe Livin' Youtube channel and play the video called 'Guided Meditation to Feel Oneness & End Suffering'. This video will guide you through the meditation. I hope you enjoy it.

TOPIC 3 - A WORLD OF ILLUSIONS

We have established in the previous topics that there is only oneness, awareness, consciousness, God that exists. With this revelation, we will now start to discuss the implications of this long-kept secret. If you are all that exists, that must mean that the world you see around you where there seems to be many different separate beings and bodies is just an illusion. And it is believing in this illusion of separation that causes all the suffering that people experience in this world.

When someone believes they are separate from other people, they are then motivated to simply look out for themselves and not care too much about others. This is what leads to selfishness, corruption, hatred, greed, jealousy, lust and war. When someone believes they are separate from the world around them, they always feel like a victim to life. When someone only believes in the material world of separation, they spend their whole life trying to achieve materialistic goals. When someone believes that they are a mind, body and character that is separate from everyone else, they believe that they can die, and they go about life with the permanent subconscious fear of death. When someone believes they are separate from the planet they live on and the animals and plants of that planet, they do not treat the planet, animals and plants with love and respect.

All this suffering is created because we have strayed so far from truth and have believed in the illusion of separation. It therefore follows that in order to alleviate all suffering, we must remember the truth of oneness and dissolve all illusions of separation created by our minds. Virtually all religions teach you that salvation comes from seeing through the illusions of the world you perceive:

Gnosticism is the teaching based on gnosis - the knowledge of transcendence arrived at by way of interior, intuitive means. Gnostics believe that humans are caught in a predicament consisting of physical existence combined with ignorance of their true origins, their essential nature and their ultimate destiny. To be liberated from this predicament, human beings must strive for gnosis. Gnosticism embraces numerous general attitudes toward life: it encourages non-attachment and non-conformity to the world, an attitude of "being in the world, but not of the world"; a lack of egotism; and a respect for the freedom and dignity of other beings. One needs also to remember that knowledge of our true nature is withheld from us by our very condition of earthly existence. In the Gnostic Gospel of Thomas, Jesus said that human beings must come by gnosis to know the ineffable, divine reality from whence they have originated, and where they will eventually return. This transcendental knowledge must come to us while we are still embodied on earth. Not all humans are spiritual and thus ready for gnosis and liberation. Some are earthbound and materialistic beings, who recognise only the physical reality. Others live largely in their psyche (minds). Such people have little or no awareness of the spiritual world beyond matter and mind. However, over the course of many lifetimes, humans eventually progress from materialistic slavery to spiritual freedom and liberating gnosis. In the fullness of time, every spiritual being will receive gnosis and will be united with their higher Self, thus becoming qualified to enter the Pleroma (heaven).

In ordinary life, we are not aware of the unity of all things - we divide the world into separate objects and events. This division is, of course, useful and necessary to cope with our everyday environment, but it is not a fundamental feature of reality. It is an abstraction devised by our discriminating and categorising intellect. To believe that our abstract concepts of separate 'things' and 'events' are realities of nature is an illusion. Hindus and Buddhists tell us that this illusion is based on avidya, or ignorance, produced by a mind under the spell of maya (which means perceiving reality without the unity of Brahman underlying all forms). Hindus believe that as long as we confuse the myriad forms of the divine lila (the creative play of the Divine) with reality, without perceiving the unity of Brahman underlying all these forms, we are under the spell of maya. Maya is the illusion of our perception when we think the shapes and structures, things and events around us are realities of nature, instead of realising that they are concepts of our measuring and categorising minds. In Mahayana Buddhism, the intellect is seen merely as a means to clear the way for the direct mystical experience, which Buddhists call the 'awakening'. The essence of this experience is to pass beyond the world of intellectual distinctions and opposites to reach the world of acintya, the unthinkable, where reality appears as undivided and undifferentiated suchness.

In both Christianity and Islam, it is believed that this earthly life should be used to worship God, follow his commandments and attempt to live without sin in order to gain entry into the ideal afterlife of heaven. People who learn to put their love and trust in God, instead of in worldly things, find a deep sense of peace and serenity that overshadows the evils, anxieties and disappointments of life, and the fear of death. In the book of John in the Bible, it says "Do not love this world nor the things it offers you, for when you love the world, you do not have the love of the Father in you." Would it tell us not to love the world if the world was true reality? The Bible says that a deep sleep fell upon Adam, and nowhere is there reference to his waking up. The world has not yet experienced any comprehensive reawakening or rebirth.

Sufis believe that man in his ordinary state of consciousness is literally asleep ("and when he dies he wakes," as Mohammad said). He lives in a dream, whether of enjoyment or suffering - a phenomenal, illusory existence. Only his lower self is awake, his "carnal soul". Whether he feels so or not, he is miserable. But the situation can potentially be changed, for ultimately man is not identical with his lower self. Man's authentic existence is in the Divine; he has a higher Self, which is true. Imprisoned in the cage of the world, man is exiled and forgetful of his true home. To keep his part of the Covenant, to be faithful to his promise, he must set out on the Path from sleep to awakening.

Plato, a Greek philosopher, used a tale of prisoners in a cave. As the story goes, these prisoners spent their entire lives chained up in a cave in such a way that all they could see was the cave wall in front of them. They couldn't see a fire that was glowing behind them, nor that a group of actors were holding up puppets and casting shadows on the wall of the cave. For these prisoners, their entire world consisted of those shadows. One day a prisoner was released from the cave and taken outside. At first blinded by the light, after a while his eyes adjusted to the brilliance, and for the first time he saw the vibrant colours and depth of real reality. His former ideas about the world were shattered, and when he was allowed to return to the cave, he excitedly explained to the other prisoners that their shadow existence was an illusion. There was a richer, intensely luminous world just a few steps outside the cave. But regardless of what he said, or the arguments he used to try to convince them that their reality was a pale cartoon of reality, the other prisoners thought he had gone mad. Plato used this tale to argue that there was a difference between the everyday appearance of the world, shaped by everyday language and concepts, and the world itself. Common sense provides a poor copy of what is really out there, so to grasp the true nature of reality requires a special form of knowing, called gnosis. Knowledge gained through gnosis is different from intellectual or rational knowing. Gnosis is a type of deep intuition, a means of knowing that transcends the ordinary senses and rational thought, like knowing from the heart.

What all these religions and philosophers are telling us is that we are asleep because we are imprisoned by our perception of a material reality. The world of separation is all we can perceive, and it is this perception that causes our suffering and misery, and keeps us from salvation. In science terms, we are focusing on the material world and ignoring 99.99999% of reality which is comprised of the zero point energy field. We must therefore be in some kind of deep sleep, a kind of deep trance, if we are oblivious to the great majority of reality. However, at any time, we can make the choice to wake up from our ignorance to discover our true nature and the true reality of the oneness of the universe.

Our Senses Deceive Us

In the last topic, we introduced the findings of quantum physics which explains how there is no such thing as matter, there is just a zero point field of energy and possibility. In fact, scientists have found that if all the (what we term) physical matter in the universe is condensed together, it would form a ball the size of a pea. Can you believe that?! It would be the heaviest pea ever, but it would be tiny. However, our body's senses and brain perceive the opposite; a world of separation and matter. How can this be?

Matter is not a fundamental property of physics. Einstein's equation, $E=mc2$, is simply a recipe for the amount of energy necessary to create the appearance of mass. It means that there aren't two fundamental physical entities – something material and another immaterial – but only one: energy. Everything in our world, anything we hold in our hands, no matter how dense, how heavy, how large, on its most fundamental level, boils down to a collection of electrical charges interacting with a background sea of electromagnetic and other energy fields. Mass is not equivalent to energy; mass is energy. As Einstein put it: "What we have called matter is energy, whose vibration has been so lowered as to be perceptible by the senses. There is no matter".

So if atoms simply consist of energy, why can't we walk through closed doors? What gives matter its solid aspect?

Quantum theory has shown that an atom's electrons can behave as either an energy wave or a "solid" particle. If there is someone that is observing the electron, it acts as a particle, but if no one is observing the electron then it behaves as an energy wave. When behaving as particles, these electrons are confined to a small region of space within the atom, and so it reacts to this confinement by moving around; the smaller the region of confinement is, the faster the particles move around in it. The tighter the electrons are bound to the nucleus, the higher their velocity will be. In fact, the confinement of electrons in an atom results in enormous velocities of about 600 miles per second. These high velocities make the atom appear as a rigid sphere, just as a fast rotating propeller appears as a disc. It is very difficult to compress atoms any further, and thus they give matter its familiar aspect.

So we now know why atoms look solid, but why do they feel solid? Well, again, quantum physics has come to the rescue here and it explains how two electrons cannot occupy the same quantum state - this is known as the Pauli exclusion principle. Therefore, the electrons in your hand can't occupy the same quantum state as the electrons of a table, making the table feel solid.

The Eastern terms of chi, or prana, are used to denote the vital breath or energy animating the cosmos. Like the quantum field, chi is conceived as a tenuous and non-perceptible form of matter which is present throughout space, and can condense into solid material objects. When the chi condenses, its visibility becomes apparent so that there are then the shapes of individual things. When it disperses, its visibility is no longer apparent and there are no shapes. This matches the findings of quantum physics of how all "matter" is just condensed energy.

What all this science is telling us, and what Hindus and Buddhists have been saying for thousands of years, is that when we focus on a material reality, we are only focusing on a very tiny portion of the universe, ignoring the one zero point field that connects everything. There are multiple energy waves we cannot see, for instance wi-fi, microwaves, and radio waves. In fact, visible light only forms about 0.0035% of the whole electromagnetic spectrum. There are multiple sounds we cannot hear, and forces that we cannot feel. But who we truly are is one with the universe, one with all these energies, one with all that is. That infinite mind is therefore filtered by the brain into a manageable experience in order to exist in a physical body. Our body's senses and brain must filter out the majority of reality, and only decode a tiny fraction of the energy waves around us to make us believe in matter and separation. This is all part of the One Infinite Creator playing hide and seek with itself.

New Models Of True Reality

The oneness of the universe is an extremely hard concept for the mind to understand because one must go beyond the mind to truly understand oneness. However, there are new models of the Universe that can make the perception of oneness a little easier to understand:

1) Holonomic Brain Theory: Karl Pribram, a professor at Georgetown University, showed that the brain is a highly discriminating frequency analyser. He demonstrated that the brain contains a certain envelope, or mechanism, which limits the otherwise infinite wave information available to it, so that we are not bombarded with limitless wave information contained in the zero point field. When we look at something, we don't see the image of it in the back of our heads or on the back of our retinas, but in three dimensions and out in the world. It must be that we are creating and projecting a virtual image of the object out in space. This would mean that the art of seeing is one of transforming. In a sense, in the act of observation, we are transforming the timeless, spaceless world of interference patterns into the concrete and discrete world of space and time. If we are projecting images all the time out in space, our image of the world is actually a virtual creation created by our minds. In essence, this model is saying that all of creation is just God's dream.

2) Holographic Universe Theory: Many physicists believe that the universe is actually a hologram. Every tiny part of a hologram contains the whole picture, which gives it its 3D look. This, in my opinion, is the best way to explain how we are both part of God and contain the whole of God within us. We are like the tiny parts of the hologram, each of us contain the whole of God, but each of us chooses to play out a unique manifestation of God, and collectively we all make up God. This is what is meant when it is said that we are made in the image of God. This is described well in the book of Romans in the Bible when it states, "For as in one body we have many members, and the members do not all have the same function, so we, though many, are one body in Christ, and individually members one of another."

3) Fractal Universe: A fractal is a type of geometrical pattern, like the one shown below. Whenever you zoom into a fractal, you find the same geometrical pattern. Basically, it is saying that the universe is like a giant Russian doll. The giant clusters of galaxies are arranged in a similar pattern to those of individual galaxies, to solar systems, to cloud patterns, to things like snail shells, to even the atom. In the last topic, we showed how the cosmic web looked very similar to our brain neural system. This is another type of fractal. Essentially, this too says that each part of the whole pattern of creation contains the whole pattern.

Like dreams, holograms and video games, the universe is created to appear real. But the dreamer is not separate from the dream. Everything is happening in oneness. To our true divine selves, the world is an illusion, but to our individual character that we are playing (our ego), the world seems real.

How To See Past The Illusions

How can we see past the illusions of separation and matter, and end the suffering we are experiencing in this dream? Well, in Hinduism, to be free from the spell of maya means to realise that all the phenomena we perceive with our senses are part of the same reality. It means to experience, concretely and personally, that everything, including our own self, is Brahman. This experience is called moksha, or liberation. One of the best ways to do this is to grow in knowledge through meditation of Brahman (oneness) to realise that circumstances in life are not real, that selfhood is an illusion, and that only Brahman is real.

In Buddhism, the Buddha prescribed the Eightfold Path in order to alleviate the suffering created by one believing in, and clinging to, the illusions of the material world. The first six sections of this path are basically concerned with releasing your attachments to the world and not taking what happens around you too seriously. The last two sections of this Eightfold Path explain that with 'right awareness' and 'right meditation', one can directly experience the mystical truth of reality.

Gnosticism viewed the central importance of gnosis as a way of directly perceiving higher states of being. The Gnostics taught that we are like the prisoners chained up in Plato's cave. That is, we have a spark of the divine within us, but we're unaware of it. Fortunately, even though we fell from grace, we can work our way back up by attaining gnosis of our true being. In this way, the Gnostics provide a way to escape from the chains of ignorance and the suffering of the material world. We can be like Plato's prisoner who escaped from the cave. The best way to achieve the state of gnosis is to hold the desire for knowledge of oneness while in meditation. You can also ask the help of the 'Messengers of Light' to help you escape the illusions.

If one is constantly investing their energy in the material world, the material world will be all they know. However, if one withdraws investment of their energy from the illusory material world, they will eventually be able to experience the truth of oneness. We have the power to see beyond the illusions outside of us merely by seeing beyond the illusions within us first. With meditation and self-enquiry, we can slowly peel away the layers of illusory disguises that we previously identified with in order to eventually discover the truth of who we are. Once you discover this truth, you will realise that this idea that you are separate from the world around you was just a figment of your mind's imagination, and that you are everything and everyone. Having experienced the truth from within yourself, you will then be able to go out and interact with the world with the underlying knowing that all is one.

A sure way to know if you are perceiving illusions at any one time is to check how peaceful, joyful and relaxed you are. If you are not so peaceful, joyful and relaxed, it is a sign that you are too attached to the material world around you and are taking these illusions too seriously, and so you feel dense. However, if you are feeling quite peaceful, joyful and relaxed, it is a sign that you are not so attached to the illusory material world and are not taking life too seriously. This course is all about dispelling the illusions of your perception of the world, one bit at a time. Upon dispelling all illusions, you will perceive true reality. This is the journey of the spiritual awakening.

Topic 3 Exercises

Day 1

Take 15 minutes out of your day today and close all sensory input from the outside material world. So wear a blindfold to block any sight, put in earphones to block out any noise, breathe through your mouth in order to not be able to smell, and sit or lie still so that you do not feel anything. Notice how taking away the ability for the illusory material world to distract you helps you come to know oneness more. However, you will realise that your mind's thoughts will continue to try to distract you. Going beyond your mind's thoughts is the last hurdle to know the truth.

Day 2

Today is all about following the Buddhist way to end suffering. Take some time to close your eyes and think about what things you are currently attached to in their present form. Perhaps you are attached to your material possessions, like your house or car? Perhaps you are attached to how your partner looks? Perhaps you are attached to your current job? You know you are attached to something because if that thing changed or was no longer in your life, you will feel sad. What the Buddhists are saying is that the material forms in life are always changing because they are illusions, and like we have said, all falseness changes; what is true can never change. So by attaching to the material forms of things, we will undoubtedly feel suffering when those forms change or cease to exist. This means you may no longer have your material possessions, your partner will age and not have the same looks anymore, or you may be fired etc. You would suffer in those instances because you are so attached to those things in their present material form. However, this does not mean that you can't enjoy material things; it just means that you recognise that material forms are illusions that will eventually change.

Day 3

For 15 minutes today, close your eyes and try your best not to think about anything outside of you. This includes other people, your problems, or things you need to do later. As far as you're concerned, these things don't exist. The only thing that exists during these 15 minutes is you. If this feels uncomfortable at first, ask yourself why? Is it the exercise that is making you uncomfortable or is it the mind's resistance to this exercise? Notice the mind's attempts to distract you from just being, by perhaps telling you that this exercise is boring or too hard. If you don't allow yourself to be distracted by the thoughts, you will feel peaceful. Oneness, or awareness, is already there within you, but these thoughts that are generated by your mind that believes in separation is what distracts you away from seeing the truth.

Day 4

Any time that you feel dense or experience negative emotions, take 5 deep breaths and say to yourself the following phrase: "This is all just an illusion". Keep repeating the phrase until you feel at peace and no longer dense. Then continue with your day.

Day 5

As regularly as you can today, remind yourself that you are dreaming. Notice how this reminder affects how you feel throughout the day.

Day 6

For 15 minutes today, close your eyes and visualise that you are a fish living in the ocean. You could be doing anything or going anywhere, use your imagination. Whatever shenanigans you get up to is allowed. Just keep visualising yourself as a fish in the ocean and do not get distracted by other thoughts. How does it feel to swim and be in the ocean? What does the ocean feel like as you swim through it? Now open your eyes – this is exactly what real life is. You are swimming in the sea of the zero point field. You are daydreaming the things around you and the things you come across in your life, just like you daydreamed in this exercise.

Day 7

Today, I would like you to go on to the 'High Vibe Livin' Youtube channel and replay the video called 'Guided Meditation to Feel Oneness & End Suffering'. Notice if you are able to go deeper into the meditation this time around.

TOPIC 4 - WHAT'S YOUR VIBE?

Nikola Tesla, who was one of the most brilliant minds in human history, once said, "If you want to find the secrets of the universe, think in terms of energy, frequency and vibration." What was he talking about? In the topic about Oneness, we discussed how the basic building blocks of the universe are atoms, almost 100% of which are composed of a zero point energy field which connects all things in the universe. We also discovered that it is the electrons that give matter its physical feel and look. But as we discussed, electrons are just energy whose vibration has been so lowered to appear as physical matter. Dr Walter Russel discovered that matter is a collection of trillions of bound photons (light) forming a giant 3D structure, or a particle. Photons circulate inside their particle in either clockwise or counterclockwise orbits. Particles with clockwise-only photons are called electrons, particles with counterclockwise-only photons are called protons, while particles with a mixture of clockwise and counterclockwise photons are called neutrons. So, in reality, light is the make-up of all matter. Therefore, the only two things that actually exist are awareness and light. Without light, there is no creation, just still, silent, dark, empty awareness. Without awareness, there is no one that can create. Both awareness and light are needed for creation. Light energy is a lower-dimensional form of the zero point energy. It is a form of energy that was brought about from awareness to enable awareness to create and experience its creations. In other words, as the book of John in the Bible says, the story of creation started when God said "let there be light".

Beings of Light

We are all the One Consciousness, but in order to play different characters, this One Consciousness has used light to create the illusions of different mind-bodies. These are the individual characters that we have been playing. If this is true, surely there is scientific evidence to prove that we are beings of light, right?

Masaki Kobayashi from the Tohoku Institute of Technology actually managed to photograph the dim glow of humans using an incredibly sensitive camera, able to detect the dimmest of lights. The stream of 'biophotons' (light from biological systems) isn't just a reflection of body heat as you may have first suspected. An infrared camera showed that some of the hottest body parts, like the side of the neck above the collarbones, give off very few photons, and the total light emissions didn't match variations in body temperature in any meaningful way. Professors Vadim Backman, Hao Zhang, and Cheng Sun backed this research up by discovering that macromolecule structures in living cells do, in fact, naturally fluoresce. They discovered that, when illuminated with visible light, the molecules get excited and light up well enough to be imaged without fluorescent stains. What this research is saying is that we actually glow in the dark – amazing!

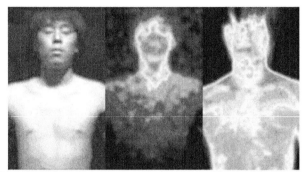

**Centre picture shows light intensity while the
picture on the right shows heat emissions**

Fritz-Albert Popp, a theoretical biophysicist at the University of Marburg in Germany, grew cucumber seedlings, which are among the easiest of plants to cultivate, and put them in his photomultiplier machine. The machine picked up that photons, or light waves, of a surprisingly high intensity were being emitted from the seedlings. Some argued that this had something to do with chlorophyll. So Popp decided that, in his next test, he would grow some potato seedling plants in the dark so that they could not undergo photosynthesis. Nevertheless, when placed in the photomultiplier, these potatoes registered an even higher intensity of light. It was impossible that the effect had anything to do with photosynthesis. Upon further experimentation, he discovered that light was being emitted from all living cells, including human cells.

This light energy has also been called 'orgone energy' by Wilhelm Reich, MD, a psychoanalyst. He observed orgone energy as a bio-electrical charge whose flow within the body could be visibly seen as waves passing through his clinical patients as they were experiencing intense emotional breakthroughs. Later, to confirm his visual observations, Reich was able to objectively measure the movements of this energy by using a very sensitive millivolt metre with sensors attached to the body to record subtle bio-electric charge.

Fields of Energy

Light is electromagnetic energy, so because we are beings of light, we have an electromagnetic energy field around our bodies which extends about five yards out. This field has often been called an "aura". When Wilhelm Reich was studying bions (short for biophotons), he also observed that when red blood cells are looked at in an alive state, an energy field is visible around them. Similarly, the Italian physicist Renato Nobili collected experimental proof that electromagnetic frequencies occur in animal tissues. In his experiments, he found that the fluid in cells holds currents and wave patterns and that these correspond with wave patterns picked up by EEC readings in the brain cortex and scalp. Even celestial bodies such as stars and planets, as well as crystals and rocks, have all been found to have electromagnetic fields.

Harold Saxton Burr, a professor at Yale School of Medicine, mapped the electromagnetic field around a single nerve. His careful measurements showed a field much like iron filings around a magnet – you may remember those experiments in school. The field was strongest closest to the nerve and became weaker moving outward from the nerve. Burr's huge insight was that fields weren't just produced by living organisms, but that fields created matter, providing lines of force around which matter could arrange itself into atoms, molecules and cells. In his book The Fields of Life, Burr used the analogy of iron filings. If you shake the iron filings off the paper and add new ones, they arrange themselves into the same patterns as the discarded ones. It is the field that is organising the filings, and so the energy is organising matter. This is why, for instance, when you cut your finger, your skin regrows with exactly the same cells and is arranged in the exact same fingerprint – the information from your field provides the blueprint around which new cells organise themselves.

Each person's energy field, or aura, is different because we are all emitting different frequencies of light. Claire Sylvia wrote a book called A Change of Heart, where she talked about her experiences after receiving a heart and lung transplant in 1988. All she knew at the time was that her new organs came from an 18-year-old male donor who had died in a motorcycle accident. After the transplant, the 47-year-old professional dancer and choreographer developed cravings for chicken nuggets, French fries, beer, green peppers, motorcycles and Snickers bars, none of which were foods or activities she had enjoyed before. Her personality also changed – she became more assertive and more confident. When Sylvia eventually tracked down the family of her donor, she discovered the foods and activities she had craved after the transplant were indeed the young man's favourites, and her new personality attributes matched that of the donor as well. That vital information was stored in the light field of the organ.

Similarly, there was a famous case where an 8-year-old girl received a heart transplant from a 10-year-old girl, after which she began having vivid nightmares about being murdered. The donor had been murdered, and the perpetrator had not been caught. The patient's mother took her to a psychiatrist who was convinced that the girl was dreaming about events that had actually occurred. They contacted the police, who opened an investigation using the girl's detailed account of the murder, including information on the time and place of the crime, the weapon, the physical characteristics of the criminal, and the clothing the murderer was wearing. The killer was identified, arrested and convicted. So in these cases, the information in the energy field surrounding the transplanted organ changed the expression of the energy field of the individual once the person had a transplant – its different light and different information mixed with the transplant patient's pre-existing field. The recipient can pick up on that information as memory in the field, and it influences their mind and their body. The energy, holding specific information, is influencing matter.

All organisms, including humans, communicate and read their environment by evaluating energy fields. In a study published in the prestigious journal Science, a research team investigated the electromagnetic relationship between flowers and the bees that pollinate them. They found that bees can detect the fields around flowers and use the information to determine which flowers have the most nectar. The ability to perceive electromagnetic fields has now been measured in algae, worms, ants, insects, anteaters, platypuses, and hummingbirds. Research has recently shown that dolphins are able to detect electromagnetic fields, and are sensitive to even very weak electrical currents.

Have you ever noticed the beautifully synchronised movement of schools of fish and flocks of birds? There's no leader, master plan, or supercomputer coordinating these millions of intricate movements. Organisation arises spontaneously, synchronised by nature. This happens as a result of information being sent and received through electromagnetic fields. Otherwise, the birds or fish wouldn't be able to communicate as efficiently, and they would end up bumping into each other, like how people bump into each other in a crowded high street. Spontaneously arising order is also evident in the functioning of our cells. Each cell undergoes around 100,000 metabolic processes per second. Groups of millions of cells, sometimes in distant regions of the body, coordinate their activities. They use energy fields to do this.

Synchronised flock of birds

Fields are a far more efficient method of coordination than chemical or mechanical signalling. Remember how old TVs were controlled by walking up to the TV and pressing its buttons? This is the mechanical approach. But now we have remotes to control the TV from the comfort of our sofa – this is the field approach. It's much faster to press the button on your remote and use the field approach instead.

Because humans are so dependent on spoken and written language, we have neglected our energy-sensing communication system. As with any biological function, a lack of use leads to atrophy. However, there are those who are a lot more sensitive to energy than others. And I'm sure most of us have at least at one point walked into a room and felt the weird or tense energy as a result of friction or disagreements between the other people in the room. Interestingly, aborigines can sense water buried deep beneath the sand, and Amazonian shamans communicate with the energies of their medicinal plants.

Meridian Points

To ancient Eastern traditions, all of this is not new information. According to the theory of traditional Chinese medicine, the human body has a meridian system running deep in the tissues of the body through which flows an invisible energy which the Chinese term as 'chi', or life force energy. Chi supposedly flows to deeper organ structures, providing energy (and thus the life force). According to Popp, the meridian system may work like wave guides, transmitting particular bodily energy to specific zones. Orthopaedic surgeon Dr Robert Becker, who performed a great deal of research on electromagnetic fields in the body, designed a special electrode recording device which would roll along the body like a pizza cutter. After many studies, it showed up electrical charges at the same places on the bodies of every one of the people tested, all corresponding to Chinese meridian points.

There has been a lot of other scientific research proving the existence of the meridian system. Previously, scientists used a combination of imaging techniques and CT scans to observe concentrated points of microvascular structures that clearly correspond to the map of acupuncture points created by Chinese energy practitioners in ancient times. In a study published in the Journal of Electron Spectroscopy and Related Phenomena, researchers used contrast CT imaging with radiation on both non-acupuncture points and acupuncture points. The CT scans revealed clear distinctions between the non-acupuncture point and acupuncture point anatomical structures.

Current Korean researchers now believe the primo-vascular system is, in fact, the physical component of the Acupuncture Meridian System. And it has also been suggested that this system is involved in channelling the flow of energy and information relayed by biophotons (electromagnetic waves of light) and DNA. The Korean scientists studying oriental medicine with biophysical methods injected a special staining dye which coloured the meridians. By injecting the dye onto acupuncture points, they were able to see thin lines. These did not show up at non-acupuncture point sites where there are no meridians. The researchers discovered that the meridian lines are not confined to the skin, but are in fact a concrete duct system through which liquid flows, and that this liquid aggregates to form stem cells. And as we know, stem cells are used by the body to transform into any cell depending on what cells the body needs at any one time.

What Does Our Inner Light Do?

Reich found that we replace used-up orgone energy by eating foods which break down into bions (particles of light from a biological system) through digestion; by breathing that takes in orgone energy directly from the atmosphere into the lungs and blood; and through the skin which absorbs orgone energy, especially when exposed to sunlight. These sources refuel the energy at the biological core.

Light, of course, is present in plants as it is the source of energy used during photosynthesis. When we eat plant foods, we take up the photons and store them. Say that we consume some spinach. When we digest it, it is metabolised into carbon dioxide and water, plus the light stored from the sun and used in photosynthesis. We extract the carbon dioxide and eliminate the water, but the light, an electromagnetic wave, must get stored as energy doesn't just disappear. When taken in by the body, the energy of these photons dissipates so that it is eventually distributed over the entire spectrum of electromagnetic frequencies, from the lowest to the highest. This energy becomes the driving force for all the molecules in our bodies. Photons (which are particles of light) switch on the body's processes. Popp found with experimentation that molecules in the cells would respond to certain frequencies, and that a range of vibrations from the photons would cause a variety of frequencies in other molecules of the body. He concluded that biophotons appear to communicate with all the cells of the body instantaneously in a synchronous wave of informational energy. Biophotons may represent a complex cell-to-cell communication that relies upon speed of light transmission. Light is the most efficient and fastest mediator of information in the material world. Light waves allow the body to manage complicated feats with different body parts instantaneously, or do two or more things at once. These biophoton emissions provide a perfect communication system to transfer information to many cells across the organism. Russian Nobel prize winner Albert Szent-Gyorgyi has suggested that protein cells act as the semiconductors of this communication system, preserving and passing along the energy of electrons as information.

An important study 40 years ago by Oxford University biophysicist C. W. F. McClare calculated and compared the efficiency of information transfer between energy signals and chemical signals in biological systems. His research revealed that energetic signalling mechanisms, such as electromagnetic frequencies, are 100 times more efficient in relaying environmental information than physical hormones, neurotransmitters, growth factors, etc. This isn't surprising though – in physical molecules, the information that can be carried is directly linked to a molecule's available energy. When chemical coupling is used to transfer their information, this leads to a massive loss of energy due to the heat generated in making and breaking chemical bonds. As a result, there is only a small amount of energy left, which limits the amount of information that can be carried as the signal. We know that living organisms must receive and interpret environmental signals in order to stay alive. In fact, survival is directly related to the speed and efficiency of signal transfer. The speed of electromagnetic energy signals is 186,000 miles per second, while the speed of a diffusible chemical is considerably less than one centimetre per second. Energy signals are a hundred times more efficient and infinitely faster than physical chemical signalling.

The Link to DNA

Popp observed that biophotons seemed to originate from DNA and is concentrated in the DNA of the cell nucleus. Accordingly, light can be stored in DNA and released over time. A particularly gifted student of Popp talked him into trying an experiment. It is known that when you apply a chemical called ethidium bromide to samples of

DNA, the chemical squeezes itself into the middle of the base pairs of the double helix and causes it to unwind. The student suggested that, after applying the chemical, he and Popp try measuring the light coming off the sample. Popp discovered that the more he increased the concentration of the chemical, the more the DNA unwound, but also the stronger the intensity of light. The less he put in, the lower the light emission. He also found that DNA was capable of sending out a large range of frequencies, and that different frequencies seemed linked to different functions. If DNA were storing this light, it would naturally emit more light once it was unwound. These and other studies demonstrated to Popp that one of the most essential stores of light and sources of biophoton emissions was DNA. DNA must be like the master tuning fork in the body. It would strike a particular frequency and certain other molecules would follow. It was altogether possible, he realised, that he might have stumbled upon the missing link in current DNA theory that could account for perhaps the greatest miracle of all in human biology: the means by which a single cell turns into a fully formed human being.

Dr Glen Rein conducted many experiments that showed how conscious intention and different frequencies of light can influence DNA. He proposed that DNA functions as an antenna, which senses subtle energies in the environment and converts these subtle energies into conventional electromagnetic energy that is then radiated from the DNA to produce a variety of intracellular events at the biochemical level. Therefore, DNA is an antenna that receives higher-dimensional light energy from its environment and transforms it into the frequencies of light that is used by the physical body.

Additional evidence for the DNA antenna model comes from some recent unpublished research with DNA at the Russian Academy of Science by Dr Poponin, who is a quantum physicist, and is recognised worldwide as a leading expert in quantum biology. In the experiment, Poponin shone mild laser light on a sample of DNA placed in a tiny quartz crystal container. The DNA was then observed with equipment that enables the observer to see single photons of light. What Poponin claimed to have found was that the DNA acted like a sponge and absorbed the light. It stored the light in a corkscrew-shaped spiral. Co-investigator in the research, Dr Peter Gariaev, concluded that DNA has a light, or energetic, duplicate. As humans have trillions of DNA molecules in the bodies, it is valid to conclude that the human body also has an energetic duplicate. This has often been termed as the 'light body' among spiritual communities. Gariaev also conducted a different experiment where he shined a gentle laser beam through a developing salamander embryo and redirected it into a developing frog embryo. This caused the frog embryo's DNA to completely re-code itself with the instructions to build a healthy adult salamander, even though the two embryos were in hermetically sealed containers and only the light was allowed to pass through. Therefore, the frequencies of light that our DNA is exposed to is what tells our bodies what to do – DNA is therefore the middle man between our light body and physical body.

Vibration Affects Matter

So far, we have discussed how we all have an inner light, whose information is stored within our DNA, and is directed around the body and outside it through electromagnetic fields along meridian pathways. But why is it important to know this? Well, since energy affects matter, not only does your personal energy field affect your physical body, but it also affects the world you perceive around you.

When you put fine sand on a metal plate and create vibrations and frequencies (perhaps by playing an instrument), the sand arranges into patterns. Different vibrational frequencies produce different patterns in the sand. This was discovered by Ernst Chaldni, a German physicist and musician.

The effect of different frequencies on sand

Water can also be made to change shape in response to vibration. When water comes out of a tube, the shape of the stream is round. If certain frequencies are played nearby, however, it changes its regular form into a series of right angles or a spiral.

When you pass sound waves through a dish of water, different frequencies create different patterns in the water. Certain types of classical music produce complex and beautiful patterns in the water, while other frequencies, such as those found in harsh music, produce chaotic and disorganised wave forms.

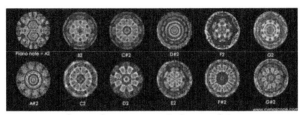

A large group of students participated in an experiment at the Aerospace Institute in Germany, where each person filled a hypodermic syringe with water and squeezed a series of droplets onto a microscopic slide. Photographs of the droplets were then taken. What they found was that each person's group of droplets looked quite different from the droplets produced by the others. The droplets produced by the same person, however, were all virtually the same. It seemed that passage through the energy field of a person produced a consistent impact on the matter, in the form of water, that they handled. It showed that the energy field of each person is unique.

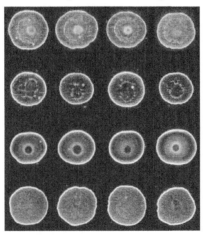

The rows show the droplets from the same person all looked the same. However, the columns show that different people had different effects on the water.

Thoughts & Emotions

These experiments show us that our energies are affecting the matter around us, and that each person's energy field affects the matter around them in a different way to another person's energy field. This has profound implications. We now know that we are beings of light energy, and we also know that vibration affects matter. Our thoughts and emotions are forms of energy that we project out. The source of these mental and emotional energies must be our inner light, or chi, because energy cannot be created or destroyed, only transformed. Therefore, our thoughts and emotions must affect the matter around us.

A study on the effects of distant intention on water was conducted by the Institute of Noetic Sciences. A group of 2,000 people in Tokyo focused positive intentions on water samples inside an electromagnetically shielded room. Unknown to the group of intenders in Tokyo, similar water samples were being held in different locations as controls. Photographs of ice crystals formed from both sets of water were then viewed by 100 independent judges. They found the shapes in the treated water more beautiful than those in the untested water. They performed even more experiments that showed how negative intentions created less appealing crystal patterns.

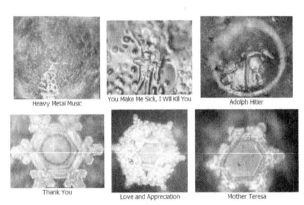

Heavy Metal Music | You Make Me Sick, I Will Kill You | Adolph Hitler

Thank You | Love and Appreciation | Mother Teresa

Dr Emoto found that different thoughts produced different water crystals

Not only is the energy we emit determined by our thoughts, but also our emotions. The vibrational frequencies of emotions are on a vertical dimension of contraction and expansion relative to the vibrational voltage of a particular emotion. The higher the vibrational frequency, then the higher the expansion, and the greater the life force in your cells. The lower the vibrational frequency, then the greater the contraction, and the less life force in your cells. For example, joy has a high frequency of 540 Hz and is a great expansive energy. The vibrational frequency of anger is 150 Hz and is contractive.

We are all beings vibrating at different frequencies, and your unique frequency depends very much on your beliefs, thoughts and emotions. As we have discussed before, believing in a world of separation is what causes us to experience negative thoughts and emotions, and is therefore what lowers the frequency of our own personal energy field. When you emit negative energies, it affects the world around you, and you end up having a negative experience of life. However, when you come to know the true nature of reality, which is oneness, the more positive thoughts and emotions you feel, and so the higher the frequency of your personal energy field. When you emit positive energies, it affects the world around you, and you end up having a positive experience of life. From this, we can conclude that to end suffering and have a better experience of life, one must come to know the truth of oneness. This matches what we talked about in the last topic in that salvation comes from shifting your focus from the ever-changing, impermanent material world, and instead whole-heartedly seek oneness, or the God within you and all of reality. Put another way, to increase your vibration, and therefore to experience true and permanent happiness, peace, joy and love, you must transcend the material world. We are not saying here that one should ignore the material world in order to increase their vibration, but to realise that there is much more to reality than what your senses can perceive.

Topic 4 Exercises

<u>Day 1</u>

This week's exercises are all about helping you sense energies. Qigong or Tai Chi are exercises involving gentle movements that stimulate the proper flow of chi, or life force energy, around your body. Today, I would like you to do a Qigong or Tai Chi session. You can find your own guided video or you can choose one of the videos in the playlist called 'Best Qigong Videos' on the 'High Vibe Livin' Youtube channel. Enjoy the exercises and notice any weird sensations as you do them.

<u>Day 2</u>

Today, whenever you experience any emotion, whether it is positive or negative, I want you to stop and focus on how that emotion feels in your body. Become familiar with what each emotion feels like.

Day 3

It might take a few tries of Tai Chi or Qigong before you can properly feel your chi, so try another Qigong/Tai Chi session today. Remember to look out for any strange sensations, perhaps any tingling sensations in your hands. This sensation is your chi.

Day 4

As you go about your day today, try to feel how the different energies around you affect how you feel. Notice the differences in energy between the different places you find yourself in. Does the energy in a meeting room feel different to the energy outside in the fresh air? Does the energy inside your house feel different from the energy at the gym? Really tune in to your surroundings.

Day 5

Again, I would like you to try another Tai Chi/Qigong video session today. Hopefully you are finding these sessions relaxing. Are you beginning to really notice your chi now?

Day 6

Today is all about noticing the energies of other beings.

As you come across people, animals, rocks and plants during your day, try to sense what their energies are like. Can you feel the difference in energies between different beings? Go outside and try to sense the energy of a plant or tree. Perhaps notice how the energy field of that tree or plant feels stronger the closer you are to it.

Day 7

Take around 10 – 15 minutes today to close your eyes and slow down your breathing. Imagine you are a great white light. You are not your body but a bright white light, like a candle in a dark room. Now, with each inhale, increase the radius of your light with your intention. So, as you keep breathing, feel your light expanding further and further out into the world. Next, with each breath, feel your light slowly contracting and coming back in. Keep gradually fluctuating between contraction and expansion of your light. Notice how this contraction and expansion feels in your body.

TOPIC 5 – YOU CREATE YOUR REALITY

In the previous topic, we discussed the notion that we affect the world of "matter" around us with our energy. In this topic, we expand on this notion and discuss how we create our own reality.

Your mind tunes in to the reality that it wants to see. It does this by ignoring what it doesn't want to see, and focusing on what it does want to see. Your mind chooses to see the things that reaffirms the beliefs you have about yourself and the world, and it chooses not to see the things that do not reaffirm your beliefs. In this way, your mind filters your experience of life based on your beliefs. For example, I used to think that I was such an unlucky person that every time I wanted to cross the road, a huge line of cars would suddenly appear so that I would have to wait a long time before I could cross. Although this did happen a few times, it did not happen every time, but my mind chose to ignore the times when I would be able to easily cross the road without cars being in the way. It works in a positive way as well - you may know of certain people who seem to always have the best luck. Life always seems to work out perfectly for them. But if you inspect closely, they are likely to just be very positive, optimistic people. If you believe you are unlucky and life is cruel, you prevent yourself from ever putting yourself out there in life, and you simply lead an average, boring, safe but unfulfilling life. However, if you are positive and optimistic, you will regularly put yourself out there and take risks which, sometimes, will pay off and will allow you to lead an interesting, fun and unique life. It all comes from your beliefs and perspective and as nothing to do with luck.

Collapsing the Wave of Possibility

Let's look at some scientific evidence which proves how our beliefs create our reality. Quantum physics has showed that the Newtonian model of an atom we all learned in school is wrong – the electron(s) doesn't orbit the nucleus in a specific known orbit. Instead, there is a cloud or field of possibilities around the nucleus – the electron is at every spot in that cloud at the same time. Each spot represents a possibility of where the electron may be at any given moment. The electrons that move around in the vast field behave in a completely unpredictable manner. They're here one moment and then gone the next, and it's impossible to predict where and when the electrons will appear. Therefore, an electron behaves as a wave of possibility. Waves carry incredible amounts of information. However, as we have noted in a previous topic, an electron can behave either as an energy wave or as a particle of matter. So what is it that makes electrons behave as a particle?

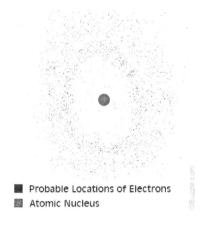

Probable Locations of Electrons
Atomic Nucleus

Quantum scientists found out, through the famous 'double slit' experiment, that we, as observers, affect how particles behave. In brief, the double slit experiment works like this: If an electron or a photon is fired through a single slit, it will appear as a dot on film. You could think of it as a bullet going through a narrow doorway and leaving a hole on the far wall. However, if you have two slits, the particle does something strange and somehow forms a wave pattern instead of a dot. If the path of the electron is knowable, they respond as particles. When we don't know their path as we don't know which of the two slits each particle would go through, they respond as waves. The scientists then decided to repeat the experiment while taking a close look to check which slit each electron went through. However, when they were observing the electron, it started to behave as a particle again. This proved that consciousness and matter are linked. It is only when an observer focuses his attention and looks for some "thing" material that the invisible field of energy and information collapses into the particle we know as the electron. That is called collapsing the wave function, or manifesting from the field of all possibilities. But as soon as the observer looks away, no longer observing the electron, and taking his or her mind off the subatomic matter, it disappears back into energy and possibility. In other words, when we expect something to occur (just like when the scientists expected the electron to behave as a particle as they observed it), we collapse all possibilities contained in reality in order to observe what we expect. And all our expectations are based on our beliefs. Yet the moment we no longer put any expectations on reality, and so not view life through the filtered lens of our beliefs, all possibilities open up to us (represented by the particles behaving as waves when no scientist was projecting any expectations). In this way, mind and matter are related in the quantum. The human observer constitutes the final link in the chain of observational processes, and the properties of any atomic object can only be understood in terms of the object's interaction with the observer. This means that the partition between the I and the world, between the observer and the observed, cannot be made when dealing with atomic matter. In atomic physics, we can never speak about nature without, at the same time, speaking about ourselves.

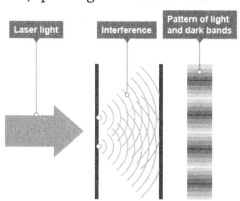

Photons behaving like waves when unobserved

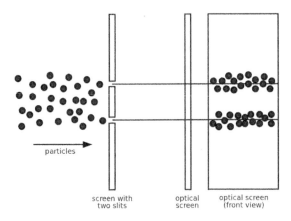

screen with two slits   optical screen   optical screen (front view)

particles

Photons behaving like particles when observed

What's more, the Institute of Noetic Studies repeated this experiment over the internet with many different participants from all over the world to study the role of distance on the results of the experiment. They tested how the particle in the lab behaved when people from different parts of the world were observing it from their computers. They found that the effects were the same regardless of distance – this proved that we even affect matter that is far away from us.

The observer effect also shows up in entangled particles. In a study using two entangled photons, each had a possible position of being either horizontal or vertical. Left to their own devices in their own little universe, the two photons remained in an indeterminate state. But when an observer intrudes on this closed system by observing one photon, the possibility wave collapses into a probability, and the photon becomes either horizontal or vertical. Its entangled partner then responds by taking up the opposite position. "In the realm of possibility", says quantum physicist Amit Goswami, "the electron is not separate from us, from consciousness. It is a possibility of consciousness itself, a material possibility. When consciousness collapses the possibility wave by choosing one of the electron's possible facets, that facet becomes actuality". So the mind, rather than impartially witnessing objective phenomena, is itself influencing which of the infinite sea of potentials winks into existence. Goswami continues, "The agency that transforms possibility into actuality is consciousness. It is a fact that whenever we observe an object, we see a unique actuality, not the entire spectrum of possibilities. Thus, conscious observation is sufficient condition for the collapse of the possibility wave."

In The Intention Experiment, her book about large international experiments that gauge the effect of human intention on physical matter, Lynne McTaggart states that the observer effect implies that "living consciousness is somehow central to this process of transforming the unconstructed quantum world into something resembling everyday reality," and that "reality is not fixed, but fluid, and hence possibly open to influence". According to Bill Bengston, "This suggests that human consciousness, individually and collectively, produces what we call 'reality'".

We don't even need to open our eyes for the observer effect to take place. Dean Radin at the Institute of Noetic Sciences set up a double slit experiment in a room shielded from electromagnetic signals and physical vibrations. Meditators and non-meditators imagined that they put their mind inside the box and were watching the photons go through the slits. The result was that the meditators were able to cause a significant shift from the wave pattern, and many particles were observed when there should only have been waves recorded. It also happens that experienced meditators were better able to cause the shift than the non-meditators, which speaks to the considerable power of the mind that can be developed through meditation. Humans did 5,000 sessions, and a computer functioning as a control recorded another 7,000 sessions. The sessions held by the computer had no effect whatsoever, but the meditators were causing a significant collapse of the wave pattern through mind power.

So what these experiments prove is that: a) mind affects matter by shaping which of its infinite possibilities is manifested, and b) distance has no impact on this effect of mind on matter. Basically, the material reality that you experiences is just your mind's projection of your beliefs. Said another way, your beliefs determine what kind of reality you tune in to out of the infinite possibilities.

The Material World is A Reflection

In the last topic, we discussed the evidence proving that our thoughts and emotions are electromagnetic energies that are emitted from within us. Your beliefs act as a program in your mind that generates most of your thoughts, and these thoughts are what trigger your emotions. Emotions are just your body's energetic responses to your thoughts. As we discussed in the previous topic, the energies you emit will have different effects on the world around you based on the frequency of those energies. If your project high-frequency energies, i.e thoughts and emotions based on love, peace and joy, you affect matter in such a way that you create a more beautiful material reality. However, if you project low-frequency energies, i.e. thoughts and emotions based on anger, fear, and guilt, you affect matter in such a way that you create a more chaotic and ugly reality. In this way, the material world that you experience is just a reflection of the energies you are sending out through your thoughts and emotions. In the book of Galatians in the Bible, it says "for whatever a man sows, he will also reap". This is telling us that the energy and frequency that we send out (sow) will be reflected back to us (reap). It really is that simple.

The Science On Intentions

Let's look at an experiment that was conducted to test the power of intention. This particular experiment was done by a French scientist called Rene Peoc'h, who demonstrated this with newly hatched baby chicks. When chicks hatch, they usually imprint on their mother, bonding with her and following her around. But if the mother isn't there when the chicks hatch, they'll imprint on the first moving object they encounter. For example, if a chick first sees a human, it will follow the human around in the same way. For his study, Peoc'h built a special type of random event generator, which is a computerised robot that would turn randomly as it moved around an arena, going right 50% of the time and going left 50% of the time. As a control, he first recorded the robot's path in the arena with no chicks present. He found that, over time, the robot covered most of the arena equally. Next, Peoc'h exposed newly hatched chicks to the robot. As expected, they imprinted on the robot as if it was their mother and followed it all over the arena. After the chicks had imprinted on the robot, he removed them from the arena and put them in a cage on one side, where they could see the robot but not move toward it. What happened next was astonishing – the intention of the baby chicks to be near to what they believed to be their mother (in this case the robot) actually influenced the random movements of the robot. It no longer moved all over the arena but instead remained in the half of the arena closest to the chicks. Peoc'h carried out a similar study with baby rabbits. He placed a bright light on the moveable REG that the baby rabbits found repulsive. When the data from the experiment was analysed, it appeared that the rabbits were successfully willing the machine to stay away from them. If the intentions of baby chicks and rabbits can influence the movements of a computerised robot, just imagine what you can do in manifesting your intentions and desires.

Figure 16.1 The path traced out by the moving robot in experiments of René Peoc'h. A: A control experiment in which the cage was empty. B: An experiment in which day-old chicks imprinted on the robot were kept in the cage. (Reproduction courtesy of René Peoc'h)

A: Shows the random movement of the robot when the cage was empty

B: Shows the movement of the robot when day-old chicks, that imprinted on the robot, were kept in the cage on the right.

Dr Tiller, a Professor in material science and engineering at Stanford University, studied mind over matter phenomena. His experiments have repeatedly shown that the power of the human mind can have a direct impact on physical matter. Working with experienced meditators who were, as he described them, "highly inner-self directed people," Tiller asked them to focus on "imprinting" specific intentions on electrical devices. For example, in one mind over matter experiment conducted by Tiller, a group of individuals put their awareness on an electrical circuit which contained a crystal. They then implanted an intent that the pH of water would either go up or go down. The circuits were wrapped in aluminium foil and shipped overnight to a lab across the country, turned on, and set beside a water sample. The room was isolated so that people did not enter, and all environmental factors of the room were carefully monitored. Despite the precautions, the water samples did respond exactly to the mind power as the meditators intended. PH rose or fell according to the intentions by a full 1.5 pH. The odds against this happening by chance are a million to one. Dr Tiller also discovered that, over time, his experiments affected the room where the experiment was conducted, demonstrating even further the power of mind over matter. The object was imparting its qualities to the room so that water placed in the room after the device was removed still affected its pH. Another of Tiller's mind over matter experiments successfully demonstrated that intention caused fruit flies to grow 15% faster than normal. He explains that mind and matter are not limited by distance or time.

Lynn McTaggart, an American journalist, author, and publisher, conducted experiments with thousands of people from 80 countries. As many as 10,000 people were involved in a single intention experiment, based around the concept of mind over matter. She started with the idea of showing that human intention affected matter. The first target was to be a leaf, and there was another leaf as a control. The intention of the experiment was to see if people could cause the leaf to glow. The group chose which leaf to work on with the flip of a coin. All living things emit photons, and with a sensitive enough camera, you can actually see any living matter glow as it emits bio-photons. Dr Gary Schwartz from the University of Arizona ran this experiment. The result was that the leaf that received people's intention glowed far brighter than the leaf that did not receive intention. This mind over matter test was successfully repeated many times. Another experiment was to see if intention could make a plant grow faster. A large number of people in Australia sent energy to seeds. The charged seeds did indeed grow faster. In yet another test of mind power, there was one experimental group and three control groups of plants. All four sets were planted. They found that the seeds that had the intention had sprouted soonest and grew fastest. In one of these experiments, the seeds even grew twice as tall as the controls. This was repeated with many large groups around the world, all demonstrating the possibility of mind over matter.

The Science On Beliefs & Expectations

An experiment that was designed to test how negative beliefs can affect your reality was conducted by Helmut Schmidt. Schmidt designed a simple machine that was based on a binary system (a system with two choices: yes or no, on or off, one or zero). In this case it would give heads or tails. Left to its own devices, it would show heads 50% of the time and tails 50% of the time. Schmidt gathered participants and created an experimental atmosphere that might encourage failure. His participants were asked to conduct their test in a small dark closet where they'd be huddled with the display panel. Schmidt avoided giving them the slightest bit of encouragement. He even told them to expect that they were going to fail.

Not surprisingly, the team had a significantly negative effect on the RNG. Their results were 49.1% in the direction of their intention. In statistical terms, this was a result of major significance; 1000 to 1 that the result had occurred by chance.

But what about positive beliefs? Researchers at New York University found that romance-minded students who believed they would get a date were significantly more likely to do so. Golfers who were told that they were playing with a lucky ball scored better during putting practice. In games of chance, optimists win more prizes than pessimists. According to psychologist Richard Wiseman, people who see a silver lining around dark clouds, using their minds to positively reframe negative events, "expect the best outcomes, and these expectations become self-fulfilling prophecies".

In an influential 1963 animal trial at Harvard University, researchers tested the expectancy effect - if you expect something to happen (or believe it will happen), you're more likely to perceive it happening. Professor Robert Rosenthal gave students two groups of lab rats. He told them that one group had been specially bred to be good at running mazes, or "maze bright". The others had been bred to be "maze dull". In reality, the rats had been randomly allocated between the two groups. The students conducted their tests and duly found the "maze bright" rats to outperform the others. Rosenthal then performed a similar experiment with teachers. He told them that tests showed that certain of their students were entering a year of academic flourishing. In reality, these students had also been selected at random. At the end of the year, the IQ scores of the designated students were higher than the control group. Mind had produced matter, with belief making significant changes in performance in the material world.

The Cleveland Clinic's Wellness Program has found that 80% of the thoughts the average person has in a day are negative – no wonder many of us are experiencing negative lives. If you're viewing life from the same level of mind every single day, anticipating a future based on your past, and holding on to the same limiting beliefs, you are collapsing infinite fields of energy into the same patterns of information, ensuring you experience a predictable, dull and repetitive life based on your past experiences. However, as the above experiments prove, by having more positive beliefs about the world, your life and yourself, as well as being optimistic and having positive intentions, you actually allow yourself to experience a more positive reality. I can tell you from my own experience that before my spiritual awakening, I was always experiencing so many issues and challenges in my life, and life seemed so dense, serious and dull. However, after reprogramming my mind and consciously choosing to have more positive thoughts, the reality I experience has become so beautiful. I rarely experience anything negative or challenging anymore, and I enjoy every minute of life. I did not suddenly just become lucky as soon as I spiritually awakened. This is not a coincidence. The change in my external reality came from first changing my internal reality.

Conscious manifesting

While more positive beliefs and thoughts improves the general experience we have of reality, can we actually manifest something specific that we want to experience in our lives? The answer is yes, but we would first have to leave the realm of what is already manifested and enter the realm of all possibilities. To experience the true nature of reality which is oneness or consciousness or infinite possibility, one must take all attention off the illusory material world and transcend the mind. This is best done in meditation. Then, from that state of total awareness where all possibilities exist, one can consciously choose what reality they wish to experience in the material world by using their mind to visualise what it is they want to experience. Remember, when in a state of awareness, all time collapses and there is only the present moment. So when visualising what it is you want to experience, you must visualise it as if you are experiencing it right now. If you visualise as if you are looking into the future, this means you are not in the realm of all possibilities that is pure awareness. This is explained in the book of Mark in the Bible when it says, "whatever things you ask for in prayer, believe that you have received them, and they will be given to you."

To scientifically test this, the Institute of Noetic Sciences conducted experiments with a computer-simulated baseball pitch (throw). It was designed in such a way that the ball never lands exactly at the centre line, it will end up either a little to the left or a little to the right. Before getting any subjects, they tested the simulation and it turned out 50-50 chances of going either left or right; and so the computer generated random results. They then gathered participants to use their intention to make the ball curve more in one direction. However, the participants did not know about the ball pitch – they were told to focus on the intention of hearing a particular phrase from the computer. The phrase would only be heard if the ball swerved in the direction the experiment was designed to test. So, say the experiment was to test if the ball would swerve to the right more with intention, they would set the computer to play the particular famous phrase whenever the ball swerved to the right, and would make the sound of a click if the ball swerved to the left. The participant would then focus with the intention to hear the famous phrase as many times as possible. They conducted the experiment many different times with many different participants, testing out both directions. They found that the average results were that the ball swerved in the direction of the intention of the participants 56% of the time - this may not seem a very significant rise, but the probability of this happening by chance was 1000 to 1. The experiment showed that when you focus on something that you wish to experience in the present moment, the material world will change in order to match your desire.

How to Create

Based on the knowledge discussed in this topic, and based on my own personal experience, here is a step-by-step guide on how to manifest something specific in the material world:

1) Enter the realm of all possibilities – To enter this state, one must take all attention off thoughts and the material world and just sit as awareness during meditation. In this state, all possibilities exist right now, and you can simply focus your attention on what you want to experience.

2) Brain Coherence – When you have aligned with the field of all possibilities, you must then solely focus on the reality that you want – but remember, visualise as if you are already in that reality now. Do not allow yourself to get distracted by any thoughts or anything else; just visualise what you want to experience. This is because the degree you are able to solely focus on what you want to experience is directly correlated with the power of your intention to manifest. This is well portrayed by lasers. A laser is set up so that all the light rays from it are parallel to each other rather than going off in random directions. This characteristic, called coherence, makes lasers extraordinarily powerful. Light from a 60-watt incandescent light bulb can faintly illuminate objects two to four metres away. It converts only about 10% of its energy into light, and that light is not coherent. Organise the same 60 watts of light into a coherent laser, however, and it can cut through steel. An ordinary handheld laser pointer of the kind used in lectures, with a tiny power source of just five thousandths of a watt, can illuminate a point 12 miles or 20 km away. Mental coherence is similar. When our brain waves are coherent, the quality of thought they produce is focused and efficient. So by ensuring that we focus on nothing but the particular reality that we want, our brain waves become coherent, sending a strong intention to the universal field.

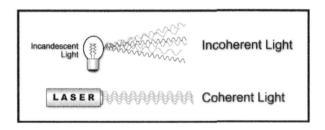

3) Use the heart - Even though the brain has an electromagnetic field around it, by far the strongest electromagnetic field in the body comes from the heart. The electromagnetic field around the heart is 5,000 times powerful than what the brain produces. Specific thoughts and intentions are generated by the mind and are used to frequency modulate the coherent bio-fields from the heart. This means our thoughts trigger our emotions. Researchers at the HeartMath Institute discovered that when one is in a state of love, the coherence is enhanced and the biofields become stronger. When you are in a state of love, you are using the strongest magnetic tool you have to attract the reality you have visualised. Therefore, it is important to only visualise things that you would love to experience; the things that would bring you joy. If you are trying to visualise something that does not bring you much joy or that you wouldn't particularly love to experience, the energetic intention of your attempts to manifest will be very weak.

4) Release - A series of experiments at the University of Edinburgh in the 1970s and 1980s used random number generators (RNGs) to explore mind-matter interactions. Participants were asked what kinds of mental strategies they used and which ones produced the best outcomes. The most successful participants reported that a key factor was the paradoxical concept of "effortless striving". This means you must absolutely want the desired outcome more than anything you've ever desired but, at exactly the same time, you must also maintain zero anxiety about it. Therefore, once you have used the above first three steps, you must completely let go of the outcome and not think about it anymore. This is because, when manifesting, you are tricking the mind into believing that you are actually experiencing what it is that you want to experience right now. However, after finishing your visualisations, if you start doubting and questioning whether your visualisations are going to materialise, you reduce that belief in your mind, which decreases the likelihood of your visualisations manifesting. So, simply release control of the outcome and trust that it will manifest. You can think of it as if, during your meditation, you have travelled to the future and seen what it is you will experience.

5) Be Patient - The most common pitfall people fall into when they try to manifest is that they give up far too quickly. While some things can manifest pretty quickly, many things can take days, weeks, or sometimes a year or two to manifest. In the grand scheme of things, this is not a lot of time to wait. If you really want something, you should be able to wait that long. However, most people for some reason expect things to manifest instantly, and if they don't, they give up and they say that manifestation is nonsense. Continue to use this step-by-step guide and just be patient. Your manifestations are coming, even if it seems like a long shot now. Life will surprise you if you just give it a chance.

In this course, I am only divulging information that I have experienced as truth and tested out for myself. To this date, I have manifested each and every thing that I have attempted to manifest, no matter how unlikely I thought it'd be at the time. This is not fantasy - I can tell you that I have personally used this knowledge to experience the reality that I want to experience, and now you can too. I want to tell you about the first time I tested all this out. As I was starting my spiritual awakening, I had about £5,000 in savings. My friend encouraged me to invest it in a fund that claimed that they had never made a month of losses and have been getting 4% returns per month for its investors. I thought "Wow, this is an incredible opportunity", and so I invested my savings. I made a month of decent gains, so my girlfriend and I decided to book return flights for a 3 month travelling holiday around the world as we felt like we were on track to get a lot of money by the time we would set off. After all, what could go wrong in four months? However, the fund suddenly lost all my money within a week, and it turned out to be a really dodgy scam. I had lost all my savings and, worse yet, we only had four months until we were supposed to go travelling. To add to this, I wasn't getting much income at all from my business at the time. What was I supposed to do? However, as I had already come across information that told me how I can consciously create any reality that I desire, I thought that this was as good an opportunity as any to really test it all out. I did not get a second job and I didn't work any harder – the only difference I made was visualising myself on the three-month holiday doing all the activities that I wanted to do. I did not want to simply get just enough money to survive – we wanted to really splash out and experience a lot during this holiday. I kept visualising it every day as if I was already on holiday experiencing those things in the present. What happened next was unbelievable. In those four months before travelling, I was getting more new clients for my business than ever, and opportunities to make extra income from minimal effort started coming my way. I eventually made enough money to have the dream holiday we were hoping for, with some money left at the end to help with finding a new home. From then on, I have been using these techniques to manifest anything that I want.

It Doesn't Always Work

However, although this all sounds great, there are a few reasons why what you visualise may not actually manifest in your life:

1) Reality is a collection of everyone's thoughts and intentions. You may intend for something to happen but many others may intend for a different outcome. As we have learned, the universe is interconnected. For instance, if you are trying to visualise winning the lottery, there are likely going to be many others visualising it as well, which greatly reduces your chances.

2) It isn't easy to be in a state of meditation and use the aforementioned techniques to create your reality. However, like anything, the more you practice, the better you will be at it.

3) You might consciously strongly desire something, but subconsciously you may not. This conflict neutralises or even reverses your intention. For instance, you may consciously want more money, yet subconsciously you don't think you deserve it, or you do not feel that you are worthy of more money. Your subconscious doesn't agree with your conscious intention. By identifying your limiting beliefs and changing them for ones that don't limit you, you will be able to resolve this issue.

4) It is not part of your life path, or is in direct contradiction with it. We will talk more about your life path and purpose in a later topic, but, in short, we all have a direction in life that is pre-determined before we incarnate. Sometimes, you may think you want something, but it does not fit in with the agreed life plan, so it will not occur. For instance, it may be part of your life plan at this stage to move to a different city or country to meet certain people, but you are trying to visualise buying a new

home in your current city. In this case, you will unlikely be able to get a new home in your current city. Your heart is what guides you along your life path, so a good sign that something is not part of your life path is if you do not feel much joy as you are visualising what it is you want to experience.

Distinguishing Desires

With this knowledge, you can now decide whether you are to allow your ego to use your mind to consciously create a more comfortable and pleasurable life full of material possessions, or whether you allow the Divine to use your mind to create unique things that will help you enjoy life and spread love to others. Either way, the mind is just a neutral tool. However, know well that the ego's desires can only give you short-term pleasure, until it eventually desires something else. This is because fulfilling the ego's desires never truly satisfies us. It is just artificial, short-term pleasure. Many people spend a number of lifetimes just trying to fulfil their ego's desires before they realise that this does not give them the inner satisfaction that they are looking for. What will truly satisfy us is fulfilling our soul's desires. These do not feel like desires per se, but are more like longings felt in the heart. Each soul's main longing is to express love, and each soul has a unique way of expressing love to others.

There are a couple of signs which can indicate to you whether a desire is of the ego or of your soul. The best way is by asking yourself whether the thing you desire is unique or whether it is based on something you have seen before. The Divine within you, your soul, will create new unique things into the world, but your ego will create based on what it has experienced in the past. For instance, I know that no one has done a spiritual awakening guide like this book before, and so I knew that the desire to create this book was that of the Divine's. However, if I were to try to manifest a car or some money, I know these are ego desires as they aren't unique. The second way to know the source of your desire is to ask yourself where your joy lies. If you will only feel joy once the thing you visualised manifests in the material world, then this is of the ego. However, if you experience joy as you visualise and create, then this is of the Divine. Using our previous example, my joy comes from writing these books; it does not come from people buying my books and giving me good reviews. However, if you were trying to manifest a car or some money, your joy would only come once you actually get the car or money. The ego always convinces you to rely on something outside of you in order to be happy, while your soul tells you that the happiness comes from within as you create. The final way to know for sure if your desire is of the ego or of the Divine is to question the intention behind the desire. Is the intention to only benefit yourself, or is the intention to benefit all (which includes yourself and others). Continuing with our example, my intention in creating these books is to help as many people as possible with their awakening. However, if I were to try to manifest money or a car, the likely intention behind it would mainly be that I could enjoy these things.

As you spiritually awaken, you will become better at being able to tell which desires come from the ego and which come from the Divine within you. And once you see the truth, how could desires based on illusions satisfy you anymore? What you will find is that you will no longer crave material things; you will only concern yourself with real desires such as expressing love. Love is the only truth, and so expressing love is the only desire worth pursuing.

Topic 5 Exercises

Day 1

Take some time today to write down what challenges you are facing in your life. Next to each challenge, think of the possible negative belief(s) that you have that may be stopping you from overcoming that challenge. For instance, if you are in a job you hate, what beliefs are stopping you from being in a job you love? Perhaps you believe that you will not have enough money and be able to pay the bills if you pursue a job you love. Perhaps you believe that there is no job out there that you will love. I was always told by so many people that "no one loves what they do, you just have to find work and do it". This is an ingrained belief that has stopped these very same people from doing what they really want to do in life. Perhaps you believe you don't deserve a better job. Again, life is simply a mirror to your own beliefs and thoughts. Do not throw this list away once you are done.

Day 2

For each of the challenges you listed yesterday, I want you to think of what positive beliefs would help you overcome those challenges. For instance, using yesterday's example, the belief that 'I will always be financially supported no matter what' would help motivate you to pursue your dream job. You can name as many positive beliefs per challenge as you want. Repeat each positive belief you have written down, either out loud or in your head, until you truly believe them. It may help to repeat the positive beliefs while you look into a mirror.

Day 3

With this knowledge that your thoughts shape your reality, do your best to really notice the thoughts in your head as you go about your day today. When you catch yourself in thought, stop immediately and review the thoughts you just had. What were they about? Would these thoughts have a positive or negative effect on your life? Keep doing this throughout your day. Notice how many negative thoughts you have. These thoughts are limiting you and getting in the way of your enjoyment of life.

Day 4

Today, we are just going to close our eyes and try our best to enter the quantum field of possibilities. To do this, you must silence the mind and simply focus on the nothingness. This nothingness is really the zero point field of possibilities – we just can't perceive it with our senses. It can only be perceived with our awareness. Enjoy the stillness and silence of this realm. Be completely present with it. Remember, any thought that pops in your head is shaping your reality. If a thought pops up, identify whether it is based on a limiting belief or not, and then bring your attention back to the stillness. Enjoy this realm for at least 15 minutes today.

Day 5

We are going to repeat yesterday's exercise – close your eyes, silence your mind, and be present with the field of possibilities. You should see some improvement in being able to stay present with this field. Are you starting to enjoy the stillness and quiet? Enjoy this exercise for at least 20 minutes today.

Day 6

We are going to put everything we have learned this week into a meditation. Go on to the 'High Vibe Livin' Youtube channel and play the video called 'Guided Meditation for When Life Isn't Going Your Way'.

Day 7

Another meditation today. Go on to the 'High Vibe Livin' Youtube channel and enjoy the video called 'Guided Meditation To Manifest Anything You Want In Life'.

TOPIC 6 – WHAT IS GOD?

What is God? If you're anything like me when I started my spiritual journey, the word 'God' had negative connotations. Growing up in a very orthodox Christian family, God was the term used for a judging, punishing and cruel being that creates people, forces them to worship him, and then consistently tests them to see if they deserve eternal punishment or eternal rewards. But you can use any term that makes you feel more comfortable, such as the Creator, the Divine, Brahman (used in Hinduism), Allah, Source, Oneness, your Highest Self, Love, or Infinity. They are all describing the same fundamental thing. It is the one intelligence/consciousness/awareness behind the whole universe. It is the Source of everything. It is the zero point field.

We have already talked about how we are all part of God, and we all collectively make up God. When you fully understand oneness, you realise there is no separation between you and God, you and others, and you and the universe. It is all simply one being, manifesting in different forms to experience itself and learn about itself. Every being, atom, planet, star and galaxy is just a vessel which God uses to experience itself from different perspectives.

God is such a difficult concept to understand and describe. This is because words are for the mind, but to know God, one must go beyond mind. God cannot really be described by words. Any word you use to describe God will never do God justice. It is like describing the colour red to someone who has been blind all their life. God can only be experienced within one's self. It is an experience for the heart, not the mind. God cannot truly be understood by the mind. By realising your true divine nature within your heart, you can experience God. However, we cannot escape the fact that we need words to refer to God and to talk to others about God. If we cannot talk to each other about God, how can we help each other to find God within? This is the conundrum.

Let's see how religions have described God. Christians believe God is all powerful, all knowing, all loving and present everywhere. In the Bible, particularly in the book of John, God is described as spirit, light and love. God is also described as the Alpha and the Omega; the beginning and end. In Islam, the Quran describes God as eternal, everlasting, the originator, the shaper, the creator and sustainer of the universe. He is also described as the all-seer. Hinduism describes Brahman as the ultimate reality – the one supreme spirit who is the indescribable, inexhaustible, omniscient, omnipresent, original, first, eternal and absolute principle, without a beginning, without an end, who is hidden in all and who is the cause, source, material and effect of all creation known, unknown and yet to happen in the entire universe. The ordinary senses and ordinary intellect cannot fathom, grasp, or be able to describe Brahman even with partial success. The Upanishads describe God as the One and indivisible, eternal universal self, who is present in all and in whom all are present. In the Gnostic view, there is a true, ultimate and transcendent God, who brought forth from within Himself the substance of all there is in all the worlds, visible and invisible. Zoroastrianism, the oldest living religion in the world, believes in one God called Ahura Mazda, and he is also described as all-knowing, all-powerful, present everywhere, impossible for humans to conceive, unchanging, and the creator of all life. Ahura Mazda is also described as the creator, maintainer and most benevolent spirit. As you can see, all these descriptions are extremely similar to each other, and they all seem to agree that God is inconceivable to man.

Science, too, agrees with religions; in the topic about oneness, we discussed the scientific validation of a zero point field, making up nearly all of the space in an atom, but which appears as dark emptiness to the human eye. This zero point field connects everything in the universe. It is this zero point field that is the one consciousness, called God. God is both nothing and everything at the same time. God is nothing based on how we normally describe a "thing", as God is invisible and not physical. However, God is the consciousness that permeates all things in the universe, and everything emanated from God, so God is also everything.

Some may still be questioning whether God exists or not, and that's fine. It is good to question everything. Even Buddhists don't really believe in one creator, but they still do believe in tathata, which means suchness. It is sometimes understood that tathata underlies reality, and the appearance of things in the phenomenal world are manifestations of tathata. In essence, they believe in one reality that underlies all illusory forms. What really convinced me that there was a divine intelligence behind everything was the beauty and majesty of the Universe. The way our body just knows what to do all the time – from replicating itself from one cell to a full human body, to healing itself, to processing information. The way that schools of fish and flocks of birds move together in a beautifully synchronised fashion. The way the planet provides the right atmosphere for life to thrive. How plants absorb energy from the sun, and we take our energy from plants, either directly or indirectly. How carbon dioxide and oxygen are perfectly exchanged between plants and animals/humans. How water is recycled from our oceans to the atmosphere and back again through rain. How the planet is the perfect distance from the sun to enable us to survive. The way that the same pattern, based on the Fibonacci sequence (see pictures below), appears everywhere throughout the Universe. The beauty of sunsets, stars, nature, art. The different types of organisms that can survive in all kinds of environments, from the bottom of the oceans, to deep underground, to deserts, mountains and the air. The unsolved mysteries of the universe. The way events seem to miraculously line up perfectly in life through synchronicities. For me, there has to be a divine, loving intelligence behind all these things. It is too beautiful and too perfect to all be an accident or coincidence.

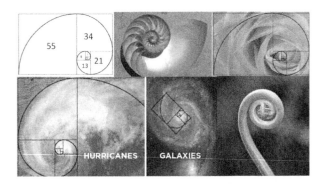

**The Fibonacci sequence can be seen
everywhere in the universe**

It is hard to understand that not only do we collectively make up God, but each one of us contains the whole of God within themselves. Perhaps the following analogies may help:

*God's VR game – One can simply view the universe and creation as one really big, long virtual reality game. While God is the only player, this one God is playing each and every character in the game simultaneously.

*God's Dream – You can view the universe and everything that happens in it as simply God having a very long lucid dream that he can control. God is the only dreamer, but God is pretending to be each character in the dream.

*God's Movie – God is creating a movie called 'The Universe', but God is the only actor, and so God must put on different disguises to appear as different characters in the movie.

*Hologram - We have already talked about how you can view the universe as a hologram projected by one mind. Each small part of a hologram contains the whole image. While there is only ever one image being projected (God), each smaller part of the hologram can be thought of as different beings playing different roles in the whole image.

*DNA – It is a scientific fact that every cell in our bodies contains all of our DNA. This means that each cell has the information within it to become any cell of the body. We all start off as one fertilised cell that contains all of our DNA; this cell then multiplies several times. Each cell then manifests only some of the information contained within its DNA to become a specific cell with specific functions. Each human body is made up of trillions of cells. So the Universe can be thought of as a human body; each being is a different cell. And so each being, planet, star and galaxy contains the information of the whole of God within it (like DNA), but only manifests a tiny part of that information to become an individual cell. Each being fulfils a different function within the whole.

As you come to know the Creator more and more on your spiritual journey, you may be able to come up with different analogies; in fact, I encourage you to do so. It is a hard concept to imagine that there is one consciousness living within us and, at the same time, imagine that we are living within that consciousness. The main thing to understand is the oneness of the universe. Remember, God has been described in religions as a spirit, or essence, within all things that cannot be detected or conceived by human senses. In science, God is the zero point field in each atom, which is invisible to us and can't be felt by us. We are not saying that God is physical matter. What we are saying is that God is the divine invisible essence (or spirit) within everything and everyone. Physical matter can be thought of as just disguises that hide the oneness and make it look like there is separation. Understanding this has profound effects on how you will treat people, animals, objects, and the planet. By treating everything and everyone as divine and one with you, you will automatically be in a constant state of love. How else would you treat other selves than with love? Could you be angry or annoyed at yourself? Could you fear yourself? No, of course not. Love is the automatic state we find ourselves in when we fully realise oneness.

Religions often teach people to spend their life worshiping and fearing God. But you are God. Why would you create characters so that you can worship yourself? And why would you fear yourself? It's nonsense. Instead, wouldn't it make sense that a loving consciousness would create in order to exchange love between all the characters? By loving anything or anyone, you are actually loving yourself. You are God and you are playing with your creative abilities to find different ways of loving yourself.

Topic 6 Exercises

<u>Day 1</u>

Today, we will look upon everything and everyone as if they are God. When talking to someone, realise you are talking to God. When cuddling an animal, realise you are cuddling the Divine. When you look at a tree, realise you are looking at God. Everything and everyone has a divine essence within them. Notice how this exercise makes you feel throughout the day.

Day 2

Make some time today to close your eyes and visualise 5 people in your life. These must be people you are perhaps angry at, or annoyed with, or scared of. Now, one by one, realise that their true essence is God. Ignore their egoic character, their false self, and realise that God is within them. They do not realise they are God, but you now do. Does this change how you feel towards them?

Day 3

We have established that your true self is in fact God. So today, we will look upon everything and everyone as if they are you. When talking to someone, realise you are talking to yourself. When cuddling an animal, realise you are cuddling yourself. When you look at a tree, realise you are looking at yourself. Notice how this makes you feel throughout the day.

Day 4

Today, make some time to just sit in a public place, perhaps in a park or on a high street, and simply observe. Observe the play of God. All the action, movement and noise that you see is the Creator playing with itself using energy. In reality, there is just stillness, silence, and nothingness, but with the illusions the Creator indulges in, it seems like there is always so much happening.

Day 5

Today, sit in front of a mirror and look into your own eyes for 10 minutes. Realise you are looking at God. The middle of your eyes appears like black, empty space, just like the zero point field. But in this blackness, in this nothingness, is your true self who is observing life.

Day 6

Whenever any low vibrational emotions, like fear or anger or guilt, arise in you today, remind yourself that you are God, you are the one true essence behind everything. You are everything and everyone. How does this reminder affect your emotions?

Day 7

When doing anything by yourself today, realise you are God who is having an experience with itself. When you are brushing your teeth, realise that you are the brush, the toothpaste, the floor, the mirror, the body. Your true self is not physical at all, but it has used the illusion of physical matter so that it can experience brushing its teeth. When you are spreading butter on your toast, realise you are the body, the butter, the knife, the toast and the plate. When you are walking, realise you are the body, the pavement, the air, the cars on the road, everything you see. Your true self is silent and still, yet it has created everything you perceive to enjoy the experience of walking.

TOPIC 7 –
TRUE LOVE

This topic is all about the love baby! If I was to ask you to describe what love is using a word, phrase or sentence, what would you say? What is love? Think about what causes love – why do you feel love for something or someone? If a stranger does something nice for you, why do you feel a sense of love? Why do you feel love towards your pet?

It's because you feel connected to them, right? The more connected you feel with someone, the more you feel love for them. And love can come in many forms, such as gratitude, compassion, empathy or forgiveness. Conversely, the less you feel connected with someone, the less love you feel for them. I remember that during the Brexit negotiations (Brexit was the term used for Britain exiting the EU), there was a special episode of 'Wife Swap' on TV. One family was pro-Brexit and the other family were EU immigrants; the wife of each family swapped places for a week. Before the swap, the family that were pro-Brexit clearly didn't understand the general situation of EU immigrants and why they would leave their country to come to the UK; you could say they were completely disconnected from the other side. Similarly, the EU immigrants had no idea why British people would vote against them. There was a clear divide between the two families at the start. Then, during the week where the wives swapped, all members of the pro-Brexit family started to know more about the EU immigrant family, how hard it was to leave their country, why they came to the UK, and how the Brexit vote is going to cause them a lot of issues. The EU immigrants also began to understand why the other family voted for Brexit. They started to sympathise and feel love towards each other; all from just spending time together and connecting. This was a clear example to me for how connection and love works.

Is It True Love?

So why do we not always feel connected to everyone? It is because we have believed in the illusory material world of separation. Even the people who we do connect with, we connect on very superficial things, such as how they make us feel, what they look like, how they act, their status or their popularity. We may even have some similarities in terms of hobbies and interests, or simply we may just be of similar ages, work in the same company or live in the same area. We connect with others based on their illusory forms rather than their true essence. But illusory forms are always changing. What happens when you or the other person change interests? What happens when their looks change, or when you have an argument with them? What if one of you moved to a different area or worked at a different company? You then start to lose your connection and so the love between you diminishes. We've all had friends who we've lost touch with and don't feel connected to anymore. This love is therefore conditional; the connection is dependent on certain factors.

When the illusory forms change, our love changes. Even your parents or siblings feel connected to you only because you have similar genes - but as we discovered in previous topics, the physical body is simply an illusory tool; it's not who you truly are. That's why many families say they love each other "because they have to"; they don't feel connected but feel obliged to love each other – does this sound like true love? In fact, all these superficial connections are made with aspects of the ego, which include the body or different parts of someone's character. The ego is the false self, and so these connections are based on illusions. That's why, despite society being more technologically connected than ever, so many people feel lonely. The connections they have aren't real. People are so separated from true love. As a result, you may notice how many people struggle to genuinely say the words "I love you" to each other, even to their own family and friends.

How do we feel true love towards others then? It's simple; you are already connected to everything and everyone as we are all one consciousness. You do not need to make efforts to form a connection; all you need to do is remember that the things that seemingly separate you from the world around you are just illusions. And this connection we all have with each other is and unconditional as this connection is permanent and unchanging. This connection is also universal as your true connection to a worm or a weed is the same as your true connection with your mother or best friend. What's more, this connection is unlimited as this connection exists between you and everything in the Universe. True love can therefore be simply defined as recognising your divine oneness with the world around you. Once you truly experience oneness, you automatically feel connected to everyone and everything around you.

Love is a topic that I believe many religions fall short on. They all tell you to love everyone, including your enemies, but they don't tell you how or why or what love even is. They tell you that you should love God above all else, which indirectly conditions you to believe that God is separate from all of creation. If love is based on connection, how can you unconditionally love God if you feel separate from God? That is why religious people say they love God when their life is going well, but are then angry at God when their life gets challenging. This is not unconditional love. Religions also fall short on emphasising the importance of loving yourself, and explaining how one can love themselves. If you are a sinner, how can you love yourself? And if you believe everyone else is a sinner, how could you love them? You cannot truly love someone or something if you view them as imperfect. You must see the perfection within someone in order to love them. You may have experienced this in the early stages of your relationship with a partner when they seem so perfect in your eyes. You may have also experienced this when you have just given birth to your baby and they seem so perfect in your eyes. Similarly, you must see the perfection within yourself if you want to truly love yourself. To see the perfection within you and others, you must recognise the Divine within yourself and others and remember that all material forms are illusions.

Love Yourself First

Loving yourself has been made to seem like an arrogant or selfish thing to do, but, in truth, you cannot truly love others without first truly loving yourself. I don't mean loving your body, or your character, but your true, divine, perfect self. To love your true self, you must first discover who you truly are, because how can you love yourself if you don't first know who you are? This involves shedding the layers of the ego, one by one. This is not easy, but, boy, is it rewarding. It is mainly done through detachment from your body and mind during meditations. Once you discover who you truly are, there is no other feeling than love that you could feel towards yourself. Permanently loving yourself becomes automatic once you remember who you truly are. In fact, you realise that you are love. Only when you have come to know who you truly are can you then go out into the world and truly love others as you will have remembered that all is one and all is perfect.

Loving Others

The biggest challenge is discovering who you truly are; once you have done that, then loving yourself and others becomes automatic. This is because, once you discover who you truly are, you instantly discover who everyone else is at the same time, as you will have remembered that you are one with everything and everyone in the universe. The same true divine perfect essence within you is within everyone else as well. So, instantly, you will love all others, and this love will be unconditional – it doesn't matter what the other may look like, or how they act, or what they say; their true divine essence is within them and never changes, whether they know it or not. And it is this divine essence that you are always one with – what feeling can you have in this instance other than love? But, again, you must look past their physical bodies and egoic characters in order to do this, much like you look past your own ego in order to discover and love your true self.

Remember, we are not talking about loving other people's

egos. You may not get on with many other characters, but you can still love their true divine selves. The ego is imperfect because it is an illusion, and so you are not expected to be everyone's best friend; truly loving someone is all about looking beyond their ego and recognising your divine oneness with them. The egos (characters) that you do get along with will likely be the ones you choose to spend more time with, such as your partner and friends. We are here to experience different characters, but to also learn that these characters are not who we truly are.

Loving Everything Else

Once you realise the one true nature of all beings, you realise this true nature/essence is also behind all trees, animals, objects, rocks, water and air. It is even within every single atom. There is one spirit, one true divine essence behind all. You then realise you are constantly surrounded by love – everything around you is one with you. When you are in love with all of life like this, you will have achieved permanent bliss, joy and happiness.

All Love is Love of Self

When oneness is fully grasped, it becomes easy to see why loving anything or anyone is a form of loving yourself. All love is self-love. When you love anything or anyone, you are loving yourself because all is one. True love is the only interaction in the world where no one loses anything – by truly loving others, you are loving yourself, and so you and the "others" both gain in love. This is why it feels good inside whenever we show love. If we are separate beings, and life is all about survival of the fittest, why would it feel good to help someone else? Logic in the material world would dictate that loving others requires some form of loss, either in material things or time or energy. However, because the material world and time are illusions, and we are in fact all connected, love is always a mutually beneficial interaction, even if the ego tries to convince you otherwise.

The ego never gives love without an intention to gain something in return. This could be appreciation, or a return of the favour, or looking good in front of others, or perhaps as a way of controlling others. And if it doesn't get what it wants from the interaction, it will think that the love it gave was a loss. For instance, if someone gives money to a homeless man, and the homeless man does not show any appreciation, the ego will feel angry because it thinks that it has lost money and not gained anything in return. This is because the ego is so focused on the material world, and ignores the loving energy that is felt from within when love is given. If someone does something nice for a friend in the hopes that their friend returns the favour, but then the friend completely forgets about this act of generosity and does not give anything in return, the ego will be angry because it will think that there has been a loss and no gain. In this way, the ego can only give conditional love, and doesn't actually enjoy the act of love, but enjoys what it can potentially get out of it in the end. In contrast, when one aligns with their true self, love is given freely and automatically because this is just the nature of who you really are. Because your true self exists beyond the material world, it enjoys the act of giving love because of the great inner feeling that this brings. The end result and gaining anything in return is irrelevant. Your true self makes no difference in the love it has for anything or anyone – it realises that it is everything and everyone, so there is no difference in the true love it feels for different people, animals, plants, or objects. It loves everything and everyone equally. Therefore, to truly and unconditionally love others, you must first align with your true self. Your state of consciousness determines the intention behind your love.

Western religions tell people that the reason they should love others is for the purpose of getting into heaven. But, again, this can only lead to an egoic form of love. This encourages people to love so that they can get something in the future. It is a sort of sacrifice they do in order to pass the test and avoid hell. They do not see the instant reward of love – by giving love, you feel love within you at the same time. You do not need to wait until you die to see the benefits of your love.

True love does not have different levels and it cannot be measured. There are not small or big gestures of true love. There are not acts of true love that have a greater impact than others. The ego tries to convince you that there are because the mind loves to categorise and measure things. But true love is beyond the mind. True love is feeling your divine oneness with something or someone, so any actions that arise while having this perception are forms of true love, and so there would be no difference between those actions in terms of energy. It is one's intention behind an act that determines the frequency of the energy of that act. Therefore, even if you do a small gesture for someone, but you do it with the intention to simply show love to another aspect of yourself, then, energetically, this would be an incredibly high-vibrational act of true love. Conversely, if you made a huge donation to charity, but you did it with the intention to gain popularity as a result, then, energetically, this love would be of a much lower vibration; a distorted, egoic, conditional form of love.

Being Yourself

You *are* love, and once you remember this, love no longer becomes an effort you make for others, but instead simply becomes an expression of your true nature. Love would no longer be an action you take, but a permanent state of being. Whenever you feel you have to try to love someone, this love is coming from the false self. Love is not the default for the ego as it is not a being of love, so loving from the ego is an effort and it is usually short-lived. You cannot truly love when you believe you and others are your false selves. Once you relinquish the ego, all you need to do is be your true self, and then everything you do will be full of love. It becomes so easy and natural at that point because love is your default. Anything or anyone can come your way in life, and you will do nothing but be in love with it all. In this way, love becomes the only thing that stays constant in your life - your surroundings may change but your state of love does not. Whoever you are with, wherever you are, whatever situation you are in, love is possible by transcending the material and recognising the oneness of it all.

Of course, it will take some time yet before you remember who you really are and are able to unconditionally love others. So are we unable to experience true love until then? You can, and the easiest way to do this is to simply look upon something or someone with no thoughts. Your thoughts are how your mind creates a separation between you and what you are looking at. But without thoughts, you are able to feel connected with whatever you are looking at. This is why children and animals just want your attention – they can feel that your undivided attention is love. Your undivided attention is your full attention without thoughts distracting you. However, what normally happens is we go through life not really giving anything or anyone our full attention. Instead, we live almost completely in the mind, and we give our attention to the ego's thoughts about everything and everyone rather than truly looking upon life with 100% focus and attention. Without the mind's expectations, or the mind's constant desire to gain something, or the mind categorising everything and putting things into a hierarchy, you are able to see the oneness of all of life. The ego's thoughts are based on the illusion of separation, so if you can look at something or someone without indulging in the ego's thoughts, you can truly love that thing or person as you will feel your divine oneness with them. Once you are able to do this, you will have had a taste of what true love is. It sounds simple but it is by no means easy. It is all about adjusting your perception so that you no longer see life through the ego's eyes. The following exercises will help you begin to do this.

Topic 7 Exercises

<u>Day 1</u>

Gratitude is a form of love. You are grateful for the things you love. So, go about your day today while trying to point out as many things that you are grateful for as possible. These thoughts of gratitude help you to feel inner love. Focus on this feeling of love as you find things that you are grateful for.

<u>Day 2</u>

Today, as you do any action, set the intention that the action will show love to another aspect of yourself. As you enter any interaction, set the intention that your words will help the other person feel great. You don't need to change what you say or how you perform an action, but just ensure there is always a loving intention behind everything you do today. Notice any changes within you as you set those intentions. Notice how your vibration changes as a result. Notice how others react differently because of your loving intentions.

Day 3

Whenever you feel anything other than love today, repeat the following affirmation: "I am one with everything and everyone". But don't just say the words; really feel them. Notice how this affirmation helps you return to the state of true love.

Day 4

Take some time today, perhaps 15 minutes, to completely focus on a being. You can do this with a partner, a pet, a plant, or even yourself in the mirror. Put your full attention on whatever you have chosen without getting distracted by any thoughts. Rarely do we look at something for so long without having thoughts. If you catch yourself in thought, bring your full attention back to whatever you have chosen to focus on for this exercise. You will notice that your love for this being will naturally grow the longer you focus on them without thoughts. It's so natural and automatic. It's so simple. You do not need to force love, it just happens when you get the ego out of the way, because this is who you truly are – a being of love.

Day 5

Any time you feel a negative emotion towards someone today, remind yourself that you are one with this person. Remember your divine oneness with them. Does this reminder change how you feel about them?

Day 6

Do you think you could ever truly love an object? Well, today you are going to see if you can. Grab an object, any object at all, and completely focus on it for 10 minutes. Make sure you do not put any focus on any thoughts - ensure 100% of your attention is on the object. Do not categorise or label the object, and do not even have thoughts about what you like about the object. Love is a feeling not a thought. Notice how your feelings about the object change as a result of this exercise.

Day 7

Today is meditation day. Go on to the 'High Vibe Livin' Youtube channel and enjoy the video called 'Guided Meditation to Experience Universal Love'.

TOPIC 8 - KARMA & FORGIVENESS

'Karma is a bitch' – we've all heard that saying. And we have all witnessed or experienced karma in action at some point in our lives. But what exactly is karma? How does it work? And how can we deal with negative karma?

We have already briefly discussed in the previous topic called 'You Create Your Own Reality' how your outer world (your external reality) reflects your inner world (your internal reality). This follows on from the principle of oneness, as you start to learn that both your external reality and internal reality are one. Therefore, the beliefs you have about yourself, others and the world will be re-affirmed back to you through your experiences. And your internal vibration will determine the general vibration of the reality you experience.

Karma is a very similar principle that is also a consequence of oneness. Karma is the reflection of your projected energy. Your projected energy does not just include your words and actions, but your thoughts and emotions towards anything or anyone are also projections of energy. The vibration of the energy your project, either via your words, actions, thoughts or emotions, will be reflected back to you in some way as a result of karma. In other words, what goes around, comes around. Therefore, if you express anger at someone through your words, you may find that other people may then start to express anger towards you. If you project thoughts of hatred on to another, hatred energy will be reflected back at you from others. If you do something nice for someone, then someone will do something nice for you. This is why, if you want to receive love from others, you must first show love to others. It always starts with you and your vibration. You must understand that you, the real you, are the only one that has ever existed, and, in reality, there are no "others". Life is just reflecting you back at you. The religious principle of 'Treat one another as you wish to be treated' is teaching us about karma. There is no separation between what you project and what life projects to you. What you do unto others will be done unto you. Even in science we know that every action has an equal and opposite reaction; this is a form of karma.

So, all those thoughts and emotions you have towards others that you think are harmless because you keep them to yourself and don't physically act upon them, they all contribute to the karma you experience. And all those times you bitched or complained about others behind their back, you were projecting negative energy that would indeed be reflected back at you at some point. There is no hiding from karma. And since your ego, which is your programmed set of beliefs, has controlled your thoughts and emotions all your life, you can see why life appears so negative. The ego's beliefs are based on the illusion of separation, which creates negative thoughts, and the resulting emotions will also be negative. All this negative energy has always been reflected back at you throughout your life, and, up until now, you did not realise that you were the one that created such a negative life for yourself by going along with your programmed beliefs and believing that you were your ego.

The issue is, karma is rarely reflected back straight away, and it is often not reflected back in the exact same form it was originally projected. It can sometimes take a few years before a projected thought or emotion gets reflected back at you, and, in some cases, karma may not even be reflected back at you in the same lifetime. What's more, the energy reflected back at you may not be in the same form that you projected it. Say you projected positive thoughts, this energy is likely to be reflected back at you, not as a thought, but as a positive material experience. This is why, when you focus more on the things you are grateful for, life will present you with more of those things as a result. Even if you, let's say, comforted a friend, the positive karma may not necessarily come back to you as a friend comforting you, but perhaps a stranger may let you go in front of them in a queue. To complicate things even further, your karmic energy may not be reflected back at you in the same number of actions. Let's say you did something really nice for a stranger, a big gesture - this may not be reflected back at you in just one instance, but it could be reflected back at you with several different people doing something small but nice for you. Because of the delay in karmic consequence, and the fact that karma is not always reflected back in exactly the same form, and that karma may not even be paid back in the same number of actions, it is easy to see why people forget or deny the existence of the karmic system. However, it is important to remind yourself that it is all about energy, and your projected energy is **always** reflected back to you, and it is always reflected back in the best possible way at the best possible time for you. Project more positive energy, and life will appear to be very generous and positive as a result. Project more negative energy, and life will seem cruel and negative.

But what is the purpose of karma? You can think of karma as a natural force of guidance, motivating you to realise your oneness with the rest of the universe, and, as a result, treat all things and people with love. Think about it for a second – what better motivation can you have to treat people with love than to know that what you do to "others" is what you do to yourself? And how else would you know that all is one if your life wasn't a reflection of you? Karma should therefore not be thought of as a punishment, but as a helpful guide. Without it, we would not have much motivation to love others, and we would not be able to realise the oneness of the universe.

Often, people seek revenge in life – when they feel wronged, they desire that the person who wronged them is punished. But what you must understand is that karma is always at work, which is the natural system that is helping everyone learn from their mistakes and eventually raise their level of consciousness. However, it is not in the sense of revenge, but as a way to guide them towards the same eventual destination as you and I; which is fully realising who we truly are. In this sense, we do not actually need a justice system. The only reason we have a justice system is because people do not trust in karma. We also have to realise that, again, they are you, you are them, you are both one. Wishing ill on them is wishing ill on yourself. Revenge, or justice (which is basically society getting revenge on someone), are often just forms of anger, and when you project anger, that negative energy will be projected back at you because of karma. Instead, see through the façade of separation and show them love, forgiveness and compassion. We will talk about forgiveness in the next paragraph, but love, as we discussed in the previous topic, is simply recognising your divine oneness with someone. Besides, many victims of crimes will tell you that getting revenge or justice doesn't usually help you, as you will still have the emotions of anger within you. The only thing that can help you is to forgive them and to project love to them instead. However, this does not necessarily mean that you should not pursue legal action against companies or people that have caused harm to you. But, before taking any action, one must fully release their anger and truly forgive the other. Then, one returns to a state of peace and love. It is only from this state of being that one ought to decide whether to take legal action or not. This is because you will be able to feel in your heart whether it is the right action to take, or whether it serves no purpose. Your true self communicates with you through your heart. However, you cannot hear your true self if you are focused on loud, angry thoughts in your mind. Furthermore, if your heart does tell you to take legal action, then, because you have already forgiven the other, you are not anxious about the result of the trial. You would not be relying on the outcome of the trial to feel better. Your higher self has guided you to take legal action for a purpose, and one should trust their higher self. However, if your heart tells you to let it go and not pursue legal action, again, you can trust your higher self that this is the best thing to do.

The Way Out

This leads us nicely on to the topic of forgiveness. If we

are truly separate beings, and life is about "survival of the fittest", why should we forgive each other? Can't we just coexist without forgiving each other? Religions will teach you that you should forgive others because "it gets you into heaven". But are you truly forgiving them if this is your motivation? Couldn't this motivation be rephrased as "if you do not forgive others, you will be eternally punished in hell"? This sounds more like a threat than a convincing argument to me. When you are forced to do something, are you truly doing it from your heart? Perhaps you may have had an incident in school or work where you had a big disagreement with a colleague or fellow pupil, and your manager or teacher forced you to say sorry to each other, shake hands and "play nice" – did you truly forgive them there and then? Were you truly sorry? Did you forget about the whole thing and carry on as if it didn't happen? I'm sure you will agree that this has never been the case.

And let us also realise that "I forgive you, but I will not forget" is a silly contradictory phrase – what does it actually mean? Why doesn't one simply say, "I forgive you" and stop there? Why does one have to add the "but I will not forget" at the end? Even if we do not verbally say this, many still think it when they convince themselves that they have forgiven the other. It just means you have not truly forgiven them. You are still holding what they did against them. In this way, you are still living in the past, rather than taking them as they are now. When one says this phrase, what one truly means is that they have suppressed their emotions of anger for now, but these emotions can come out again if the other person isn't nice to them. They use their anger as a way to force the other person to treat them nicely. To release the anger is to forget. Forgiveness simply means looking upon someone as they are now, with no regard of their past actions.

Forgiveness is only needed if you still believe in some form of separation, which is an illusion. If you are still thinking about the past, such as your previous actions or someone else's actions from the past, then this will trigger the low vibrational emotions such as anger and guilt. As we have discussed before, believing in a past and future is separating time; the present is the only time that ever exists. The past and future are simply illusions. If you are living in the present, there is never anything to forgive. Even if someone wrongs you right this second, by the time you have finished this sentence, it is already in the past. Similarly, if one truly loves another, then one can feel their divine oneness with the other no matter what actions the other may do. True love allows you to see beyond the illusory material forms. Therefore, if someone's actions affects the level of love you feel for them, you have believed in separation between you and the other, and you do not truly love them. Forgiveness is only needed if you still believe in separation. If you have discovered who you truly are, and your oneness with others and the universe, you are always in the present moment and always feel love towards yourself and others no matter what. In this way, forgiveness is a route to love and presence. By forgiving, we are then in the right state of mind to love. We cannot love someone when we are angry at them, and forgiveness is the process of releasing our emotions of anger towards someone. Similarly, we cannot love ourselves if we feel guilty or shameful; forgiveness of the self is the process of releasing these emotions.

It is only someone's ego that commits any action other than love, because our true self is love. Love is our true self's default, but it is when we associate ourselves with our ego that we do not show love. But, as we have previously discussed, the ego is an illusion. Wouldn't it be silly to get angry at an illusion? Don't you feel silly when you get really angry at something that happens in a dream, and then you wake up and realise it was just a dream? In a similar way, getting angry at the ego's actions is silly and pointless. Therefore, forgive yourself for the past actions of your ego as you did not know what you were doing. You were under a spell. And when you have forgiven yourself in this way, you are better able to forgive all others for their past actions as well, as they too have been under a spell. When Jesus was crucified on the cross, he said, "Forgive them for they know not what they do". The people that were angry at him did not know what they were doing; they were associating themselves with their imperfect egos. Even when people are killing you, you must realise that they do not know what they are doing. In terms of consciousness, those who are still associated with their egos are like babies or puppies, and how can you be angry at a baby or puppy? They just don't know any better. Every being is a different aspect of your consciousness. They are all just different forms of you. By forgiving others, you see past their illusory forms and remember that they are you.

We have all done and said things that we perhaps regret later on, so isn't it hypocritical to get angry at another for doing or saying something that was perhaps not wise or loving? None of us are perfect yet we demand perfection from everyone else, and if someone does something that isn't perfect, we get angry. Many of us demand perfection from ourselves as well and so we feel angry at ourselves and guilty if we do or say something that we later regret upon reflection. This is just more egoic nonsense. We are all on the journey to perfection; to return to being our true, perfect selves. We were not born perfect, otherwise there would be no journey. We are all here to experience and learn from our experiences. Let's give ourselves and other people a break, and let's help and support each other on our journeys rather than hypocritically get angry at each other for every single "mistake". When you see beyond all imperfect, illusory, material forms, you will be able to see your perfection and the perfection of everyone else. When you can see someone's perfection, you will never get angry at them no matter what as you will have loved them unconditionally. Therefore, forgiveness is only needed when you do not truly love someone. All forgiveness is thus the forgiveness of self for believing in illusory material forms rather than seeing the truth of oneness.

Many religious people talk about repentance without actually knowing what it means. The true meaning of repentance is to first awaken to who you truly are, and then to forgive yourself and others for what you all did when you were indulging in illusions. By remembering who you truly are, you ensure that you will never do unloving acts again because you will have aligned with your true, loving nature. This is the only way out of the cycle of negative karma. It makes me smile when people say they're sorry and won't do something again, but then they do something similar soon after. They haven't really repented; they haven't discovered who they truly are. To repent, one must know who they truly are; if not, then one will still associate themselves with their illusory ego, and the ego will continue doing unloving acts. You might say to me, "Well, you don't know what this person did to me, how can I forgive them?", or "I did something terrible, how could I possibly forgive myself?". But you must understand that everything that requires forgiveness is born from the same cause; you believing that you are your ego, or you believing that someone else is their ego. It all comes from your belief in separation. By transcending the illusion of separation and remembering the truth of oneness, you can forgive yourself and others for the past, and in so doing, you will have learned the lessons that karma has been trying to teach you. As a result, you release yourself from the shackles of any further negative karmic consequences from previous projected energy.

Topic 8 Exercises

Day 1

Today, I want you to spend some time writing down the things you feel guilty about from your past. Write it all down as a list on a piece of paper and keep this paper for tomorrow's exercise.

Day 2

For everything you noted as feeling guilty about, realise each one of those were done by your false self. They were caused by an illusion. You did not know who you truly were in those instances. And realise that the past no longer exists, only this present moment exists. It does not matter what your ego did in the past. With this knowledge, forgive yourself completely. Do not focus on whether others will forgive you, just focus on forgiving yourself for everything. It may help to say "I forgive you" out loud while looking in a mirror. If you can forgive yourself for one thing, you can forgive yourself for everything, because it is the same process.

Day 3

Take some time today to write a list of all the people you are angry at, and the reason you are angry at them. Really dig deep into your past and try to list as many as possible. Keep this list for tomorrow's exercise.

Day 4

Take the list from yesterday, and for each person and incident, realise that their actions were committed by their false selves in the past. But the false self is an illusion and the past no longer exists, so the past is also an illusion. Isn't it silly to be angry at illusions? Forgive them because they did not know what they were doing, just like when you forgave yourself because you did not know what you were doing. It may help to say "I forgive you" out loud while visualising the other person in your mind

Day 5

Whenever you feel you are getting annoyed or angry at someone today, rather than reacting immediately with any thoughts, emotions, actions or words, simply take 10 deep conscious breaths and just focus on your breathing as you do this. Impulse reactions are always done by your ego, while you are only able to respond as your true self when you are in a relaxed state. The deep breathing will help silence your irrational ego and allow you to hear the rational voice of your true self. By aligning with your true self in this way, you will find that you do not project any negative energy, and so you will not create any negative karma. Notice how your response changes as a result of this exercise, compared to what your response would have been had you allowed your ego to react impulsively instead.

Day 6

With everyone you come across today, do not listen to thoughts about their past; take them exactly as they are in the present moment. It doesn't matter who they are, view them as if you have never met them before. The person they are today is completely different from the person they were until today. Notice what difference this makes in how you feel about them.

Day 7

Today, you are a completely different person to the one you were in the past. It does not matter what you have done or who you were before today. Act and speak as if you have no past whatsoever. If thoughts pop up about the past, do not put any focus or attention on them. Memories about the past should be viewed as just dreams. It is only the present moment that really exists. How did this exercise affect how you felt during the day?

TOPIC 9 - LIVING IN THE PRESENT

This week, we are going to tackle one of the hardest challenges of any spiritual awakening; living in the present. We are all at our happiest when we live in the present. Don't believe me? Then just think about the happiest moments of your life – were you present during those moments, or were you thinking about the past or future? I am 100% confident that you were living in the present for all those moments. When you watch young children or animals, you never see them thinking about the future or past, they are only thinking about what they are doing that second. That's why they are so innocent and spontaneous, and such a joy to watch. This is what we should strive to be like. As Jesus was quoted as saying in the Bible, "Truly I tell you, unless you change and become like little children, you will never enter the kingdom of heaven. Therefore, whoever takes the lowly position of this child is the greatest in the kingdom of heaven."

If we are at our happiest when living in the present, why do we not always live in the present then? Why do we change from being young children that live in the present to adults that worry about the future and feel depressed about the past? Well, as we grow up, we develop an ego as a result of the programming we are exposed to. Animals do not have an ego, and young children have not yet formed an ego, and so they can easily live in presence. This doesn't mean we should strive to get rid of our ego; you will find that a near impossible task. The ego is part of the human experience. Instead, we must realise that the ego, which takes us away from the present moment, is not actually who we truly are, and we must return to alignment with our true self, which only resides in the now.

When you are present, you do not have to think about anything; you are just being. That is why the ego does not live in the present, because there is no use for it there. It can only think about the past or future. When thinking about past events that it deems as bad, it dwells on them, causing depression, anger, guilt, shame, and low self-esteem. Even when it thinks about good times you had in the past, it will nostalgically think of them as "the good old days", and it will make you believe that those good times are gone, making it seem like the present moment is not as good. When the ego thinks about possible bad events in the future, it causes feelings of anxiety and fear. Even when it thinks about good possible events in the future, it will come at it from the angle of things that are lacking from the present moment, causing you to feel bored and frustrated with the present moment. Therefore, there is no good that can come from listening to the ego with regards to thinking about the past or future. And according to a Harvard study, we spend 50% of our time awake not thinking about what we are actually doing – this can be rephrased as stating that we spend 50% of our day in autopilot mode. While in autopilot mode, we are taken away from the present moment as we indulge in the ego's thoughts about the past and future, but, at the same time, we are still just about able to function and perform our tasks for the day in a robotic way.

Think about how many times in the day your ego has thoughts like, "I'll be happy when I have this or that" or "If this happens, then I'll be happy". It may not be conscious thoughts, but, subconsciously, these thoughts are going on all the time in your mind. But the ego is never fully satisfied, even if it gets what it wants; it will always have a desire, and every desire takes you away from the present moment. Fantasising about the future makes you completely miss the joy of the present moment. Everything has advantages and disadvantages – that comes from duality. Ever wondered why the grass is always greener on the other side? The ego is constantly focusing on the disadvantages of what you have and the advantages of the things that you don't have. It is constantly resisting the present moment. Much unhappiness in life comes from this resistance to the present moment. It is the root cause of material desires, restlessness, boredom, impatience and loneliness. Boredom is simply not accepting the present moment and thinking you need something else to be content. Restlessness is feeling like you need to be doing something different to what you are doing now. Impatience is the desire to skip the present moment until a future situation occurs. Loneliness comes from not appreciating the joys of solitude that the present moment is offering you, and feeling like you need others around you in order to better enjoy the present moment.

Even when you are not thinking about specific past or future events, you are still subconsciously looking at life through the lens of the past. Let's do an exercise – pick something to look at in the room or place you are currently in. Try to notice the subconscious thoughts you have about that thing – you might have a thought about how you like the colour, how the object felt the last time you touched it, the last times you used that object, the smell of the object that you remember, any past experiences with that object or similar objects. Now notice how each of these thoughts make you feel – the particular colours or shape may trigger a happy or slightly depressing emotion in you, perhaps you don't like the texture or the smell. Now shift your focus to something else in the room – notice how your inner emotion has changed since you were looking at the first object. It's a subtle but nevertheless real change in emotion, and it is thoughts that trigger emotions. What thoughts and feelings do you have about this second object? Now look around the room and notice the subtle changes within you as you shift your focus to different things. The same happens with people – when you see someone you know, you might have thoughts about previous times you spoke to each other or saw each other, or the last thing you heard about them. Even when you see a stranger, you probably have thoughts about what kind of person you think they'd be, you may have opinions about their appearance or dress sense based on past experiences, or they may remind you of someone you know who you like or don't like. In this way, you are constantly looking at reality with the lens of the past. You are concentrating on what is familiar. We rarely observe without the ego's thoughts. Living in the present is all about putting your full attention and focus on either your internal state or your external surroundings without being distracted by thoughts.

The past and future do not actually ever exist. Think

about it; at this very moment, the only time you can say is truly real is the present moment. The past was previous present moments that do not exist anymore. The future is possible present moments that do not yet exist. The present moment is the only time that exists now. Think about it this way - if you were to get amnesia, your past is erased but the present moment can never be erased from you. Only illusory times can be erased. The past and future only exist in your mind when you believe in separation. The past and future are ways for the thinking mind to separate different present moments in a linear fashion, but in truth, the only time that ever exists is the present moment. When you are present, you look upon everything and everyone as completely new, even if you have seen that object before or met that person before. In this state, you take everything and everyone as they are now, without any thoughts about the past.

But how can you look at yourself and others as completely new each day? What if you did something really unloving to someone, or someone did something really unkind to you? How can you look at them brand new? As we discussed in the last topic, forgiveness is required to reach the state of consciousness of pure love, presence and oneness. By letting go of the past, you can put your full attention on the present moment. Forgiveness is only needed if you are thinking about the past. It does not matter what you or anyone else has done, what matters is right now. If people don't forgive you and are still holding things you did in the past against you, it is their problem as they have chosen to dwell on the past. Similarly, if you haven't forgiven someone completely, then you have chosen to live in the past. It is this choice, our own choice, that allows the past to still keep us in unhappiness.

Presence is the state of joy, bliss, peace and happiness. It is where nirvana, moksha, or heaven is found. That's why Jesus once said, "The kingdom of heaven is within you now". If I was to ask you, "What do you need right this second as you read this in order to be happy?", what would you say? Nothing, right? That's because you never need anything else when you are in the present moment. You always have everything you need, but not everything your ego desires. And you can go from one present moment to the next, all throughout your life, realising that you don't need anything else right now in order to be happy. Desire only arises as a result of imagining possible futures and favouring these imaginary situations over the present moment.

People often mistake living in the present as just spending all your money now and doing silly reckless things; a YOLO mentality. But this is not what living in the present is all about. When you live in the present, you are being your true self. Only your true self lives in the present - it is your ego that lives in the past and future. When you become your true self, even for a few moments, it's not like your true self is going to start doing reckless things. No, in fact, it will guide you to do the things that are right for you at the time, while also having fun along the way. Living in the present means admitting that anything could happen at any moment, and you are open to whatever comes your way. It is a total acceptance and trust that you are experiencing exactly what you need to be experiencing at all times. When people do reckless things, perhaps when they think that the world will be over tomorrow, they are still thinking about life from a future perspective; they are thinking about how the world will end in the future. When living in the present, you are telling yourself, "There may be a next moment, or maybe there won't be. It does not concern me. What concerns me is this moment right now." When you live in the present and become your true self, you are able to fully experience and enjoy what you are experiencing right now without the resistance of the ego.

Living in the present doesn't mean not planning for the future either. For instance, if you suddenly get the inner urge or feeling in your heart to start saving in order to buy a house, then this is your true self guiding you to do it. However, if you are first having thoughts of fear about the future, or thoughts of comparing yourself to others, and these thoughts lead you to think that you should start saving for a house, then this is not coming from your true self. If it is a desire arising out of fear, then it is surely coming from the ego. If you get a sudden or spontaneous inner excitement or feeling in your heart to do something, this is your true self guiding you to do it. By living in the present moment, you shift your focus away from thoughts and on to your inner feelings, and so, you are better able to hear the guidance from your true self. When living in the past or future, you are focusing on your thoughts rather than your inner feelings, and it is your ego that tries to guide you with thoughts. Your true self will always give you the guidance you need in order to make sure that your needs are always met. Therefore, there is never any need to worry about the future, as long as you remain present and follow your inner feelings rather than your ego's thoughts.

So how do we do it? How can we stay present in this world that seems to always force us to think about the past or future? Start by trying the following exercises to see which ones work for you.

Topic 9 Exercises

Day 1

What's your next thought? – Once you catch yourself in an egoic stream of thoughts, simply detach and then ask yourself "What will be my next thought?", and just wait in anticipation. What you'll realise when you do this is that the next thought doesn't come. That is because the ego requires you to be unconscious in order for its thoughts to flow easily, but this exercise forces you to be more conscious. The ego can only function as a background program in your mind. It doesn't like to be seen by your consciousness.

Day 2

Gratitude – Anytime you catch yourself drifting into thoughts about the past or future, immediately start listing the things you are grateful for in your life right now. What you will notice is that gratitude shifts your focus away from the past or future, and it allows you to enjoy the present moment more.

Day 3

Sensory Perception – At any time you catch yourself not being present, switch your focus to your senses. What can you see? What can you smell? What can you hear? What can you feel? This exercise returns you to the here and now.

Day 4

Do What You Love To Do – When we do things that we love, we are more present, but when we do things that we don't love, we easily slip into autopilot mode, which is the ideal mode for the ego to function. By spending more time doing the things we love, we can be present for a greater part of the day. So, just for today, cut out anything that you know easily allows your ego to take you away of the present moment, and only do things that you love.

Day 5

Don't be predictable – When we do the exact same things every day, it is easy to go on autopilot and get lost in our thoughts. By ensuring that our days aren't exactly the same, we force ourselves to be more present. You could do small things like changing the way you brush your teeth and comb your hair, or changing your shower routine, or mixing up what meals you have, or taking a slightly different route to work. Or you could do something new each day, like trying a new exercise class, or meeting new people at a networking event. You may even push the boat out and try an adventurous activity that you have always wanted to do. The main thing is to ensure that nothing about your day today is exactly the same as yesterday or a week ago. If you feel like doing a new activity, just go with the flow. Notice how this exercise forces you to be more present.

Day 6

Conscious breathing – A lot of our day is spent having

shallow automatic breaths, but when you intentionally focus on taking deep breaths into the abdomen, it takes your attention off the ego's thoughts and makes you more relaxed. An additional trick that I use is to focus on the gap between the in breath and out breath – it's a brief moment of peace and bliss. So, whenever you catch yourself in an egoic thought stream, bring your attention to your breath and focus on the gap of bliss between the deep inhale and exhale.

Day 7

Meditation – You can use meditation to shift your focus away from the ego's thoughts about the past and future, and you can focus on something in the present moment instead. There are many things you can switch your focus to instead, but, for now, go on to the 'High Vibe Livin' Youtube channel and enjoy the video called 'Guided Meditation to Silence the Ego, Feel Joy and Be Present'.

TOPIC 10 - TRUE HAPPINESS & DEALING WITH EMOTIONS

If you ask people what they want in life, the first thing most will say is happiness. But what is true happiness? Many of us have experienced a few moments of happiness in our lives, but is it true happiness if it doesn't last? Just as true love is permanent and unconditional, so too is true happiness permanent, unconditional and unwavering, meaning that nothing can affect it. So, if someone has achieved a state of true happiness, this means anything can happen in their life and they will still be as happy. True happiness does not depend on anything, anyone, or any situation, otherwise it would be conditional. "This state of true happiness doesn't exist" I hear you cry. But I promise you, from my own experience, I can tell you that it does.

Firstly, let me ask you to think about the happiest moments in your life – why were you happy in those moments? What triggered that happiness? How long did that happiness last? Why did that happiness eventually stop? What you'll find is that, because there was a trigger which caused your happiness, there will also be a trigger to stop that happiness. This happiness is conditional – you felt happy in a certain situation, perhaps with certain people, but when the situation changed, you were no longer happy. Your happiness is reliant on your illusory outer experiences, and because illusions always change, your emotions are always up and down like a roller-coaster, depending on what situations life presents you.

Since you can't control every outer experience you have, the only solution is to find happiness from something that is permanent and never changes. If you can do this, then you will always be happy. And what is the one thing that is permanent and never changes? Your awareness. Even though life is always changing as it is just one big illusion, your awareness is always still and silent, observing all of life. Therefore, true happiness is found from perceiving the oneness of all that is. You may remember that this is very similar to our definition of true love, but true love, true happiness, inner peace, permanent joy, and constant bliss are all just different terms describing the same thing - the state of being one is in when they have realised oneness. From this state of being, this level of consciousness, this corrected perception, it does not matter what outer experiences you have as you can see through the ever-changing illusory forms, and you can see the truth of oneness behind it all. As a result, you do not experience any ups and downs as you go about your life, but just one constant state of enjoyment.

True happiness is therefore realising that there is never any need to be unhappy because all of creation is just an illusion. How do you do this? Surely if you are in a challenging situation, this can lead to being unhappy? But is it the external situation that causes your unhappiness? Or is it your thoughts about the situation? Let me give you a simple example to demonstrate this. Imagine that your flight back home from a holiday got cancelled, and the next one back is the following day. The plane company puts you up at a hotel for the night, pays for your dinner and breakfast, and sorts out your plane tickets for the next day. One option is to react to this with thoughts of anger at the situation, worry about making it home, fear of punishment from your workplace for not returning on time, and thinking "Typical! This kind of thing always happens to me". Alternatively, the other option is to realise that there's nothing else you can do to change the situation, and that this means an extra day of holiday, free accommodation and food, and knowing that all will be fine in the end. Why does the first option lead to unhappiness but the second option lead to peace and happiness? The unhappiness in the first option couldn't have been caused by the plane getting cancelled because in the second option it was the same situation. From this example, we can conclude that it is when we listen to our ego's thoughts that unhappiness occurs, yet the ego tries to convince us that it is the external situation that triggers our unhappiness. It is the exact same story with anything in our lives – it is not the external situation but our own thoughts that get in the way of our happiness. Because the ego believes that there is nothing beyond the material world, it attaches to the illusions of the material world and cannot see the oneness of it all. When we align with this perception by believing we are our egos, we take life so seriously and get swept away with the ego's negative thoughts. However, if we detach from our egos and align with our true selves, we can see the truth behind the illusions, and we can always be in a relaxed state no matter what life brings us. This relaxed state is also the state of true happiness.

Dealing with emotions

Thoughts trigger emotions, and so, if you associate with your ego, you will experience negative emotions as a result of indulging in the ego's negative thoughts. These thoughts and emotions are what block you from experiencing your natural happy, blissful, joyful state. In fact, the only challenges we face in life are not actually what happens in our outer world; the real challenges we ever face are just dealing with our ego's negative thoughts and the resulting negative emotions in response to our outer circumstances. Your natural state is pure happiness, but by allowing yourself to be distracted from your natural state by your ego, you are taken away from happiness to unhappiness. Because our beliefs create our thoughts, and our thoughts trigger our emotions, the best way to ensure you are never unhappy is to drop all your beliefs and come to know the truth of oneness from within yourself. However, this takes time, so the next best thing you can do in the meantime is to become aware of your ego's thoughts at all times and realise that these thoughts are not yours (as we discovered in topic 1). This allows you to detach from your ego's thoughts instead of being swept up by them. However, this may prove difficult at first and it does take some practice, so the next best thing you can do if you find yourself indulging in your ego's thoughts about your external environment is to appropriately deal with your negative emotions as they arise.

Whenever we experience negative emotions, we usually

either project those emotions or we suppress them. But when we project negative emotions onto anything or anyone outside of ourselves, we create negative karma. And when we suppress negative emotions, we block our chakras, which lowers our vibration, it can cause health issues, and we become very emotionally fragile, ready to have an emotional outburst at any moment. So, what is the solution? The first thing to do when you experience a negative emotion is to realise that this emotion is only temporary, as long as you allow yourself to feel it completely. There is no need to judge the emotions as bad, but just realise that the emotion is just the body's natural energetic reaction to your ego's thoughts. Emotions are just energy, and energy can be transformed. When you allow yourself to feel an emotion, but without directing it at anyone or anything, without suppressing it, and without trying to justify the emotion, you will find that the emotion just disappears after a while. This is because bringing your awareness to your negative emotions transforms that energy into understanding and acceptance. The important thing to remember is that it is not other people or something outside of yourself that has caused your negative emotions; the cause of every negative emotion you experience is you listening to your ego's thoughts. By not blaming outside influences for your negative emotions, and by not suppressing those negative emotions, you can then allow yourself to completely feel the negative emotions until they disappear.

Emotions become suppressed when we have not dealt with them properly – instead of facing them, we judge them as bad, we ignore them, and then we try to distract ourselves, perhaps by keeping ourselves busy, looking through our phones, or by taking alcohol or drugs.

These emotional energies don't just go away; they linger within us until we deal with them properly. In essence, we postpone feeling those emotions completely, and we prolong the effects of those emotions on our lives. But suppressed emotions lower our general vibration. Since the vibration of our realities is a mirror to the vibration of our inner realities, suppressed emotions keep us in a low-vibrational reality. This mirror tries to help us deal with our suppressed emotions so that we can deal with them properly and, in so doing, raise our vibration. Therefore, if we have suppressed anger, life may present us with situations that try to bring this suppressed anger to the surface so that we can deal with it. It may seem like the world is trying to annoy you, but life is simply trying to help you raise your vibration.

When one has suppressed many emotions, they become very emotionally fragile. They can have an irrational emotional outburst at any time, in reaction to even the smallest things. It is like we have buckets of water within us, where the water is our suppressed emotions. The more suppressed emotions we have, the more full our bucket of water is. The bucket of water is balancing on a very thin pole. As our vibration is reflected back at us through the "outside" world, it is as if life is poking our internal bucket of water with a stick. Life is trying to help you get rid of all the water, because a bucket without water represents a relaxed, happy state. Life wants you to be happy. Eventually, life succeeds, and the bucket falls and the water spills. This often manifests as a big release of emotion, perhaps in the form of projected anger or a breakdown in tears. We can either be angry at life for poking our bucket with the stick, or we can realise that the reason we have water in the bucket in the first place is because we have not dealt with our suppressed emotions. By emptying our bucket appropriately, and ensuring our bucket remains empty by no longer associating with our egos, we can realise true happiness. In this way, life can keep poking at our bucket, but because we never have any water in the bucket, our happiness is never disturbed. To free our being from the shackles of suppressed emotions relating to our past experiences, we again simply need to bring these emotions to the surface and feel them completely without resisting or projecting them, and they will transform as a result.

Therefore, when life presents you with a challenge, the first thing to do is to allow yourself to completely feel any reactionary emotions until they are transformed. Once they are transformed, you will return to your natural, happy state, and from this state, you will know what actions you can take in the present moment that can help you overcome the challenge that you are facing. If there is nothing you can do right now to overcome the challenge, then there is no need to dwell on it. The ego will try to put thoughts of worry about the challenge, and these thoughts, if invested in, will trigger emotions of fear, but worrying never solves anything. The appropriate solutions to any challenge can only be found when you are in a relaxed, peaceful state, and so you must detach from the ego's negative thoughts if you wish to overcome your challenge and stay in a high vibration at all times.

True happiness can only be realised, not achieved. It is not a future goal that you need to plan and work hard for, as the ego would have you believe. True happiness is already within you and has always been within you, you just need to realise it, and you do this by disassociating and detaching from your ego.

Topic 10 Exercises

<u>Day 1</u>

Today, I want you to notice the emotions that arise throughout the day. Just notice them. Keep checking in with your body throughout the day to see how you are feeling. Are you annoyed? Are you angry? Are you scared? Or are you happy? Whatever the emotions are, notice them. At the end of the day, draw a graph that roughly depicts how your emotions went up and down during the day.

<u>Day 2</u>

Today, when you feel a negative emotion, notice what your ego tells you is the cause of your emotions. Be aware of the voice in your head. Is it saying that something or someone outside of you has made you unhappy? Notice how the ego is convincing you that you are not linked to your outside reality, and that you are a victim to life.

<u>Day 3</u>

Take some time at the end of the day to close your eyes and replay your day in your mind. Whenever a negative emotion arises within you as you replay your day, stop visualising, and simply allow yourself to feel that emotion without directing it to anyone or anything. Just be with the emotion. After this negative emotion has been transformed, continue replaying the rest of the day in your mind, and repeat the exercise for any further negative emotions you identify. Continue until you have finished replaying your day and have worked through all the negative emotions you experienced.

Day 4

Today, whenever you notice that you are experiencing a negative emotion, simply pause and allow yourself to feel this emotion completely. Do not carry on with your day until this negative emotion has been transformed. Excuse yourself from work if you have to. Once the negative emotion has been transformed, carry on with your day until you notice another negative emotion arising within you, at which point repeat the exercise. Continue with this exercise for the whole day.

Day 5

You can prevent yourself from experiencing negative emotions if you detach from your ego's negative thoughts straight away. So, whenever you experience a challenge today, no matter how small, be aware of the ego's negative thoughts relating to that challenge, and simply shift your focus to your deep breathing. Once the ego's trail of thoughts has stopped, you can carry on with your day. Repeat this exercise when you need to during the rest of your day, and notice how you experience much fewer negative emotions as a result.

Day 6

You now have practiced how to appropriately deal with emotions, both as they arise, and at the end of the day, and you have also practiced how to prevent these negative emotions from arising. Today, we are going to work on releasing your suppressed emotions. Choose the most intense, negative emotion that you have suppressed. This is usually related to some childhood trauma that you have tried to block out of your mind. Now, use this emotion for the meditation on the 'High Vibe Livin' Youtube channel called 'Guided Meditation to Help You Deal With Emotions'. Notice how you feel at the end.

<u>Day 7</u>

Today, repeat yesterday's exercise, but for the next most intense and negative suppressed emotion you have. Notice how you feel towards the incident that initially triggered that emotion within you as a result of this exercise. Do you feel lighter and happier? Feel free to use these tools and keep working on any other suppressed emotions you have until they have all been transformed.

TOPIC 11 - THERE IS NO RIGHT OR WRONG

In the last topic, we discussed how when we associate with their egos, we experience many emotional ups and downs in life. The reason for these ups and downs is that the ego creates the illusion of separation within our minds. So it may separate things into likes vs dislikes, good vs bad, right vs wrong. When the ego deems our life situation to fit into the positive categories of 'likes', or 'good', or 'right', then the ego is happy. When the ego deems our life situation to fit into the negative categories of 'dislikes', or 'bad', or 'wrong', the ego experiences unhappiness. This is why an ego-based life leads to conditional happiness and a life full of emotional ups and downs. It is the ego's illusions of separation that create duality in this world. In reality, there is no duality; there is just oneness. When you are able to see past the illusions of separation and material existence, and can feel the oneness of all that is, there cannot be right vs wrong, or good vs evil, because you can see that everything and everyone is a part of you.

We have all seen the yin yang symbol before – this symbol

perfectly summarises how both evil and good are simply two different manifestations of the same energy. Seeing duality is seeing illusions. One could see the yin yang symbol as two different symbols next to each other; one black and one white. Another person may see just one whole symbol. This is the same with life and the universe. If you are seeing separate beings, separate places, separate situations, and experiencing separate emotions, this means you are seeing duality, which is an illusion. If you see past the illusions and recognise the oneness behind all things, you will see that there is no duality, no separation. As Ra nicely put it in *The Law of One*, "In truth there is no right or wrong. There is no polarity for all will be, as you would say, reconciled at some point in your dance through the mind/body/spirit complex which you amuse yourself by distorting in various ways at this time. This distortion is not in any case necessary. It is chosen by each of you as an alternative to understanding the complete unity of thought which binds all things. You are not speaking of similar or somewhat like entities or things. You are every thing, every being, every emotion, every event, every situation. You are unity. You are infinity. You are love/light, light/love. You are. This is the Law of One."

All things have the underlying essence of love within them; it is your ego that has thoughts of "that's bad" or "that's good", or "that's wrong" or "that's right". And these thoughts are based on one's beliefs. Have you ever noticed that things society deems as bad or good change all the time? Homosexuality, holes in jeans, sex, and men talking about their emotions were all thought of as bad before, but now they are good. Black slavery, women suppression, smoking, being overweight, the death penalty, and men marrying young teenage girls were all commonly thought of as good or right before, but now they are deemed wrong or bad. Truth can never change – it is only illusions that can change, and our beliefs are based on illusions of duality. Have you noticed how a tanned skin colour is viewed as the ideal in the West, but having white skin is the ideal in the East? Have you ever met someone who some people love and some people hate? Why do we find people so passionate about different sides of an argument? Surely someone or some culture is right and someone or some culture is wrong? No, it is all based on our beliefs. Some people believe certain traits in people are good, and certain traits are bad. Some people believe their perspective on a topic is right and any other perspective is wrong.

Your judgements merely reflect your beliefs, but what are your beliefs based on? Did you come up with your beliefs on your own? Or were they influenced? What you'll find is that all your beliefs are influenced by factors such as your upbringing, education, society, culture, and media programming. They are not really your beliefs – you have simply been taught that something is right and something is wrong based on your past experiences. You have been conditioned to separate life and to create duality. But this duality and separation is all just in your mind. To spiritually awaken, one must drop all the illusions of separation so they can look on everything, everyone and every situation with no thoughts of judgement. They simply experience with the knowledge that all is one.

A common argument to this topic is: "So are you saying that other people can just do whatever they want and it's never bad or wrong?". This is a very third dimensional question. Those who ask this still cannot comprehend how there are no "others". Life is just you playing with yourself. If you were the only player in a virtual reality game, can anything you do while playing in the game really be classed as right or wrong, or good or bad? Of course not, and it is the same situation for life. Ra often state in *The Law of One* that "There are no mistakes under the Law of One." "How can there not be mistakes?", I hear you shriek. Many of the most materially successful people in the world often tell us that they have made more mistakes than anyone, and that is why they are successful. They made more mistakes but learned important lessons along the way which helped them become materially successful. And the same can be said for spiritual success. Are they mistakes if they eventually lead to desired outcomes? Without making 'mistakes', we would not learn or grow as much or as fast. And what is a 'mistake'? Why do we make 'mistakes'? Mistakes are just actions that come from not knowing who we truly are. They are actions caused by the false self, the ego, which is an illusion. But by making these so-called 'mistakes', and by learning from them, we can start to remember our true selves. If someone commits an action when they don't know who they truly are, one who is not spiritually awake will judge the person's actions, and perhaps the person, as bad. In contrast, a spiritually awakened person will see their oneness with them, and will treat them as divine and perfect no matter how they act - this is unconditional love. By not judging each other, and by treating each other with nothing but unconditional love, we can help each other grow and learn from our actions. We have an internal moral guidance system, which is our heart. Our true divine self guides us through our heart. When we begin to follow the guidance of our heart and become our true selves, we will naturally only do loving actions because we are beings of love. It is who we truly are. Therefore, is it not best to help each other discover who we truly are instead of judging each other for actions done by our false selves?

The ego creates duality in life, and then aims to only experience the 'good', the 'right, the things it likes, and the emotional ups, and it does not want to experience the rest. See how silly the ego is? Life occurs according to the Divine's will, yet the ego separates the Divine's creation into different parts, and then aims to only experience the parts of the Divine's will that it feels would be enjoyable, comfortable and pleasurable. In this way, the ego tries to control creation, but, of course, the ego will never be successful, and so, we are faced with only two rational options: 1) We can either accept that life is always going to present us with both sides of duality, the right and the wrong, the good and the bad, the ups and the downs, or 2) We go beyond the mind and see the oneness of all of life, and realise that duality and separation are just illusions created by the mind. When you can look upon any part of creation with no judgements of bad or good, right or wrong, and with no desire to control creation for your ego's personal comfort, pleasure, benefit or satisfaction, you will fall in love with all of life. And this love will be permanent and unconditional. In this state, no part of life will ever look bad or wrong to you. There is no right or wrong, good or bad; creation just is.

Topic 11 Exercises

<u>Day 1</u>

Take some time at the end of the day today to identify

any moments of the day in which you felt frustrated. Why did you feel frustrated? Did your ego judge someone or a situation as bad or good? Did your ego tell you subconsciously that "This shouldn't be happening like this"? What you'll find is that any frustration is initially caused by the ego's judgements.

Day 2

Any time you feel you are getting frustrated today, tell yourself "I have judged this situation". Just like the exercises in previous topics, this brings the focus back on you (the cause of the frustration) instead of the ego's outward projection.

Day 3

Spend some time today to think about certain times in your life where you initially deemed the situation as really bad, but then it turned out to be the best thing that could have happened. Don't those initial judgements seem so silly now?

Day 4

For 15 minutes today, close your eyes, and focus on the fact that you are the creator of your own reality. Whenever you feel frustration or a low vibrational emotion, you are always the cause. It is never caused by anything or anyone other than you. Sit with this fact. Know that you have the power to never feel frustrated and never feel low vibrational emotions, as long as you don't listen to the ego. You have complete power over your life. Sit with this knowledge.

Day 5

Today, make a list of some of the things your ego deems as wrong in this world. When you have finished, close your eyes and repeat the affirmation "I am everything and everyone. I am all there is, ever was, and ever will be." Keep repeating until you really believe it. Now open your eyes and look back at the list. Do you feel differently about those things? Now that you know you are one with all those things in the list, do they still feel wrong? You are the underlying essence behind all situations, all people, and all things in the universe. How can there be anything that is wrong?

Day 6

Today, make a list of some people that your ego deems as bad. This could be people you know personally, or celebrities, or anyone. Now, just like yesterday, close your eyes and repeat the affirmation "I am everything and everyone. I am all there is, ever was, and ever will be." Repeat the phrase until you have believed it. Now open your eyes and look back at the list. How do you feel about these people now?

Day 7

Without the voice in your head, you would not judge things. Judgements are just programmed beliefs. If you catch yourself feeling frustrated today, immediately try and identify the judgement behind your frustration. Notice how becoming aware of the underlying judgement eases your frustration.

TOPIC 12 - WHAT'S THE PURPOSE OF LIFE?

Can you tell me what the purpose of life is? Why are you here? What are you supposed to do with your life? We are about to explore these questions in a way that you probably haven't explored them before. They are some of the most fundamental questions in life, but they surprisingly have very simple answers.

Our country tells us that our purpose is to pay our taxes and to be a positive influence on the economy rather than a drain. In this way, our country values people with high salaries over those who are unemployed or on welfare. Our education system tells us that our purpose is to memorise as much book knowledge as possible and get as many qualifications as we can. In this way, it looks at PhD graduates more favourably than those who don't have any university or professional qualifications. Our employers tell us that our purpose is to contribute to their profits as much as we can. This means they value CEOs and Directors above employees such as cleaners and apprentices. Society tells us that we need to do what everyone else is doing, otherwise we will be outcasts. Our parents tell us that we need to follow in their footsteps and get a respectable job, get a house, get married and have kids. Those who do this make their parents proud while those who don't are viewed as disappointments. Western religions tell us that God created us in order for us to worship him, and to abide by strict rules or else we will be eternally punished. This means those who are more dedicated to worshiping God and live a stricter lifestyle, such as priests, are looked on more highly in religions than atheists. But do you actually believe any of this? Do you think this beautiful vast universe was created, and the miracle of your life was created, in order for you to get qualifications so that you can get a meaningless job that you don't like so that you can buy things that society tells you to buy? And would a loving God create you in order for you to worship him, otherwise he will punish you forever? Does any of this actually resonate with you? Has any of this led to true fulfilment for you? Most of us will not admit that this is what we think the purpose of our lives are because these beliefs are subconscious. Our minds have been programmed with these beliefs because this is what we learned from our upbringing, society, culture, education system, workplace, and media programming.

Notice how each of those purposes are about how you can benefit another party, such as your country, God, your workplace, or your parents. But is the meaning of your life just to please everyone else around you? Many will say that their purpose in life is to be a good parent – while this sounds nice, it is still all about what you can do for someone else; your kids. I'm not saying that all these purposes are bad, but what about you? What about what you want to do in life? Even though we have been spending our lives trying to please others, many of us feel so dissatisfied with life. We feel a longing but we don't know what for. Did you also notice how all those purposes I listed are about you having to do something in order to be favourable or valuable to another party? We always feel we have to do something, even things that we don't truly want to do, in order to feel valued and appreciated by others. There is no focus on simply being. We value people based on what they do in life – those who work long hours, persevere through struggles, and perhaps make products or services we all use, are hailed as incredible special people, but those who relax and play more in life are viewed as people who are wasting their life.

But let me ask you something - why does life have to have a purpose? What if life is meaningless? Your mind will undoubtedly feel uncomfortable and disturbed with this prospect, but deep within you there is a knowing that this is the truth. The best things in life do not have a purpose. What is the purpose of laughing with friends or family? What is the purpose of singing or dancing? What is the purpose of casually playing your favourite sport? What is the purpose of playing games? There is no purpose to all these things - life is most enjoyable when all purposes and goals are removed. With no goals or purposes, what else is there to do but play and laugh and enjoy life. In those moments that you are experiencing true joy and happiness, your ego cannot exist. So your ego creates the idea of purpose or goals, otherwise it would no longer exist. As your ego is a set of programmed beliefs, the purposes or goals it puts on life will also be programmed. Society programs your mind to have materialistic goals and believe that the purpose of your life is to please others. Your ego then pushes you to make efforts to fulfil these goals and purposes. But achieving these goals and purposes has never, and will never, really satisfy us, particularly in the long-term.

What's more, a purpose or meaning can only be put on life if you do not know that you are eternal. When you believe that there is a time limit on your life, your ego can easily create goals to achieve by the time you die. This keeps you in a state of constant tension and striving. However, if you remember that you are an eternal being then you completely relax. Why rush to fulfil any goals or purposes in life if you live forever? Your mind cannot comprehend eternity or infinity, and so your mind will be unable to create goals or put purpose or meaning on life. To remember your true eternal nature, you must realise that your ego is just a figment of your imagination. Your ego, your individual character, can die, but if you realise that your character is just an illusion, you will know that the truth of who you are is permanent, with no beginning and no end.

Whenever you put meaning or purpose or goals on any activity, that activity becomes less enjoyable. And it is the same case with life itself. To really enjoy life, you must go beyond your ego which is what wants to put meaning and purpose on life. If there is only oneness and perfection, why is there creation? Why does God create anything if there is no meaning. The answer is because creation is just God playing with light energy. It's all a play, or 'lila' as it's called in Hinduism. Therefore, you have two options of how you want to live your life. Do you continue trying to put purpose and meaning on life and constantly strive to achieve materialistic goals, or do you enjoy life and play? When you play and enjoy life, you are being your true divine self, but when you are trying to fulfil goals or purposes, you are being your false, illusory self. In Taoism, Tao literally means "the path" or "the way." It is a universal principle that underlies everything from the creation of galaxies to the interaction of human beings. It can be thought of as the play or will of God. According to Taoists, human happiness is realised when one follows the natural order, acting spontaneously and trusting one's intuitive knowledge. In the Tao Te Ching, the ancient sage Lao Tzu talks about how the foolish expend a great deal of energy and time trying to do everything and end up achieving nothing. On the other end of the spectrum, the truly wise don't seem to do much at all, and yet achieve whatever they want. This magic is possible, indeed inevitable, when one is in tune with the Tao and acts without attachments.

How do you enjoy life then? Well, simply put, you follow your heart an intuition. Instead of doing what everybody around you wants you to do, you live life according to yourself. You do what brings you joy. You follow your inner guidance and longings. This is how the Divine tries to play through you. You simply need to get your ego out of the way and not let society's programming stop the Divine from playing. The overall main longing within you throughout your soul journey will be the longing to remember who you truly are. The general trajectory of your soul journey is to remember more of who you truly are until you fully become your true, divine, perfect self. If you can't take the fact that there is no meaning or purpose to life then let the meaning of life to you be to remember who you truly are. However, just know that you are always who you truly are, you are just playing the game of forgetting and then slowly trying to remember.

But once you fully become your true self and your soul journey ends, then you will just start a new soul journey and play the game again. Again, your mind will see this as pointless, but your true self loves the fun of the game.

Topic 12 Exercises

<u>Day 1</u>

Take some time to think about the things in your life you have done because you felt like you should do them, or felt that that you needed to do them, rather than actually wanting to do those things. Why did you feel like you should do those things? Why didn't you want to do them? Did doing those things make you happy?

<u>Day 2</u>

Take some time today to think about the times in your life when you had an inner urge to do something or to pursue something, but then you never did. Why didn't you do those things? What stopped you? Do you regret it?

<u>Day 3</u>

Today, you will let your heart guide you as to what to do. Do nothing unless you get the inner urge to do something. I am not talking about urges based on you following a routine – I am talking about impulsive spontaneous urges, or urges from the heart. Do not plan your day at all or think about what you need to do; just follow what your heart wants to do in each moment. How did this change your day? How did you feel throughout the whole day? How many times did your ego try to tell you that you should be doing something else?

Day 4

Repeat yesterday's exercise. It takes practice to get into this state of being. The only thing that exists is the present moment. Do not think at all about the future, not even 1 minute into the future. This is all about taking yourself out of autopilot mode and being more conscious of your actions.

Day 5

Today, just play your favourite game or sport, for no reason other than to enjoy doing what you love. Notice how you feel while doing it. Are you joyful? Are you present?

Day 6

Today, I want you to enter each interaction today with the intention of laughing with the other person. Take things lightly and try to make jokes. Notice how this allows you to enjoy your day more. When you are laughing or playing, you are being your true, divine self.

Day 7

Take some time today to think about how the experiences in your life have all been trying to help you learn more about who you truly are. Upon reflection, what were the most significant experiences that were helping you remember?

TOPIC 13 - DISASSOCIATING FROM THE EGO

The spiritual awakening is all about disassociating from your ego, i.e. realising your individual character is just your illusory false self, in order to remember who you truly are. I have sometimes referred to the ego as the thinking mind up until now because the ego is a programmed set of beliefs within the thinking mind. It often seems as if the two are one and the same, however, in this topic, we will discuss the distinctions between the two.

The Thinking Mind

In *The Law of One*, Ra describes us as mind/body/spirit complexes that are of the third density level of experience. We are third density beings, which is the density of self-consciousness or self-awareness. This is what separates us and animals, who are second density beings. Self-awareness is the conscious knowledge of one's own character and feelings. It is the ability to be aware of different aspects of the self, the illusory individual self, in relation to the world around us. In order to be capable of such, our minds must be capable of abstract thought. Thus, the fundamental necessity is the combination of rational and intuitive thinking. The third-density mind is capable of processing information in such a way as to think abstractly, and in what could be termed "useless" ways. Ra tell us that our bodies were designed to be weaker than that of animals in order to encourage us to use our thinking mind for survival. This weakening of the "physical vehicle" was also designed to encourage us to deal with each other more, therefore "the lessons which approach a knowing of love can begin". However, because of self-awareness, a third density being can either choose to be service to self or service to others. All an animal or plant worries about is the survival of itself – its decisions are based purely on natural instinct. It doesn't need to concern itself with any others. An animal only helps its tribe because it ensures greater safety for itself. This is not selfishness as animals are not capable of being conscious of themselves in relation to others. However, in third density, we all have to deal with each other, and we all have the ability to be self-aware, which offers us the potential to be selfish (and therefore service to self) or selfless (service to others). The thinking mind is therefore part of this stage of our collective spiritual journey.

The thinking mind itself is a neutral tool; it can be used for reasoning and rational thinking. However, what it thinks about and how it is used can be manipulated. Here are some of the main characteristics of the thinking mind and how the ego, a program within the mind, uses these characteristics:

· **Hierarchy** – The thinking mind loves to put things in a hierarchy. This helped the early humans in the past by, for instance, informing them of what types of shelter are better than others, or what animals are easier than others to hunt. However, in modern society, we do not have to worry about these things anymore. Instead, the ego uses the hierarchical nature of the thinking mind to create very competitive personalities. Because it believes there is a societal hierarchy, it always wants to be as high up on that hierarchy as possible. So it wants to be the smartest, the most beautiful, the funniest, the richest, the best at something. This is why people screw each other over just to get ahead in their career, or why people are willing to do anything to be rich and famous.

· **Categorisation** – The thinking mind loves to put things into categories; for instance, bad or good, right or wrong, left or right. This was useful for our early human ancestors to survive, perhaps by understanding which types of food were good or bad for our bodies, or what animals to avoid and what animals to hunt. However, again, we do not need to worry about these things to help us survive anymore. Instead, the ego uses categorisation to create separation, duality and judgement in this world. Many wars are caused by both sides believing they are right and the other is wrong. The ego divides people into categories of rich and poor, pretty and ugly, evil and good, sinner and saint, popular and not popular. As we have discussed before, believing in separation leads to suffering and a lack of love in this world.

· **Materiality** – The thinking mind can only use the information it is given in order to create thoughts. This input of information comes from our sensory organs. Whatever we see, touch, hear, smell and taste is what our thinking mind can have thoughts about. And what we perceive with our senses is a world of separate bodies, things and places. The ego has the belief that what the thinking mind perceives by the senses is all there is, and whatever it can't perceive through the senses doesn't exist. In this way, the ego focuses on the material world; it doesn't perceive the invisible, subtle, spiritual essence behind reality.

· **Time & Space** – The thinking mind only understands things when put in a linear fashion. This is how it understands time; it separates the past, present and future. It separates time into years, months, weeks, days, minutes and seconds. In a similar way, it creates space – one object must be a certain distance from another, and to get from one place to another, it must take time. This is obviously useful for us in the modern day when perhaps planning our journey routes or using information from the past to help us make decisions that could lead to a better future. However, the ego uses this function to dwell on the past and worry about the future, taking you away from the present moment where true happiness can only be found. Time and space also further emphasise the ego's perception that everything is separate.

· **Protection** – The thinking mind can be used to protect the physical body. This was of course useful for the early humans to escape danger and to try to live for as long as possible. However, when associating with the ego, one believes they are the physical body rather than seeing it as a tool. Because the body can get sick or die, the ego is always looking to protect itself from potential harm. This constant protective attitude leads to distrust of others and anxiety about possible future scenarios. This leads to a constant state of fear. The ego also believes it is the character that it is playing. As we learned earlier, the ego likes to put everything in a hierarchy and so places the character it is playing somewhere within the societal hierarchy. Therefore, it is always trying to climb the hierarchy and protect itself against possible situations which may result in the lowering of its position in that hierarchy. This is why people get angry when someone embarrasses them or when someone attempts to exert power over them. It is also why people do not want to be seen with others who they deem as lower down than them in the hierarchy. It is the reason why people try so hard to act 'cool' and fit in. This constant state of fear leads to the ego being in a permanent state of protection.

Understanding The Ego

The thinking mind is therefore a computer; information from our senses are the inputs, our beliefs are the computer's programs, and the outputs are our thoughts. Beliefs determine the lens through which we view life. Whatever beliefs we have will determine the thoughts that we have about the world we perceive. And as we have discussed in previous topics, our emotions are the body's energetic responses to our thoughts. As we have previously learned, our thoughts and beliefs are what create our reality. Whenever we are experiencing suffering in our lives, it is because we have certain beliefs that have created thoughts and emotions of suffering. The beliefs that lead to suffering always come from the ego. It is not our fault that we have developed an ego, a false self - we live in a world that has programmed our beliefs in a way that we ignore true reality and believe we are our illusory false selves. This has been done very intentionally by certain forces and entities, but that is a story for another day. Many believe that their beliefs are completely their own, but what you must realise is that your beliefs have been heavily influenced by your upbringing, society, education, culture and media programming. They are not yours – they have been given to you by the matrix that we live in.

We are not in control of the thoughts and emotions that result from the ego's beliefs. Someone who is very identified with their ego will start off with one thought relating to something that they have perceived through their senses, perhaps innocent enough, but then the ego will lead them on an endless trail of thoughts that completely stray away from the original innocent thought. They will be in and amongst those thoughts for a long time. I'm sure many of us experience this on a daily basis – this shows that we are not in control of the thoughts that result from the ego's beliefs. And it is our thoughts and beliefs that shape our reality and influence our decisions in life. So, in this way, our false selves have been controlling our lives.

We experience the ego in order for God to experience playing different characters. In this way, God is playing hide and seek with itself, and so must separate into different beings and make the separation believable. However, over the course of our soul journeys, we all gradually remember who we truly are and dissolve all illusions of separation. We experience the ego so that we can eventually go beyond it and realise the truth. God loves this journey of remembering who it is.

Disassociating From The Ego

Therefore, the thinking mind is not evil or bad – it is a part of this stage of our spiritual progression. In fact, the thinking mind is simply a tool, a tool which can be useful to help us solve problems or materialise our creations. We may use the thinking mind to help us fulfil our duties at work or at home. But the thinking mind can be used by either your ego or the Divine within you. For example, my true self is using my thinking mind to help me communicate my truth to you through this course. But, as with any tool, the thinking mind should only be used as and when it is needed – like a calculator. However, because the ego lives in your thinking mind, its aim is to use the thinking mind to control you and your life. It doesn't want you to be sovereign of the thinking mind as then it will have no power over you. We must therefore disassociate from our ego if we want to take back control of our minds.

To disassociate from your ego, you must simply become aware of it. When you become aware of anything within you, if it is not for your highest good, it will simply dissolve away. So whenever you catch yourself having negative thoughts or feeling negative emotions, simply become aware of them. Becoming aware of something allows you to detach from it. Instead of being all among your thoughts and emotions, and being swept by their negativity, you take a step back and observe it all. As a result, you end up being a neutral observer to all the forms of energy that arise within you. While it is important to deal with the ego's thoughts and emotions, to fully disassociate from your ego, you must become aware of it at its source, which is your programmed beliefs. You must take time to analyse what the underlying programmed beliefs behind each egoic thought and resulting emotion are. Again, by becoming aware of these beliefs, they no longer have a hold on you. You see the ridiculousness of them and they can no longer fool you. By becoming aware of the beliefs that have been programmed into you, and by remembering that your beliefs create your reality, you give yourself the choice to whether you want to continue believing in the programmed belief or to believe something else. The ego can only be in control when you are in a subconscious sleep and are not aware of it. But the more you become aware of it and its effects on you, the more you return the power back to the Divine within you.

It is then up to you to consciously reprogram your mind to have more positive beliefs. When you have discovered a truth from within, this truth becomes part of your being and becomes a new positive belief. However, these do not feel like beliefs but are more like 'knowings' as they are things you have come to know from within yourself. Beliefs are things you have been taught are true by outside sources, and so they are borrowed, inauthentic 'truths'. It is therefore best to become aware of your programmed beliefs, drop them completely, and start fresh in trying to find what is true. But this time, always come to know things from within yourself rather than from outside sources. Yes, outside sources may present a perspective on certain things, but you must always go within to find out if what is being communicated resonates with you. If something resonates, i.e. you get an inner excitement when reading/hearing/watching the information, then this is the Divine within you telling you that this is your truth. In this way, you allow your heart and intuition to be your ultimate guides.

As we learned in previous topics, changing your beliefs will lead to changes in your reality. Therefore, if you replace negative beliefs, i.e. beliefs based on the illusion of separation, with positive beliefs, i.e. knowings that are based on the truth of oneness, you will create a more positive reality for yourself that is more aligned with your true nature, full of love, peace and joy. Positive beliefs lead to positive thoughts, which lead to positive emotions. This is the process for taking back control of your mind, and ensuring that your mind is only used how you, the real you, want it to be used.

The Re-enactment of Adam & Eve

We all may have heard of the story of Adam and Eve; however, what you may not know is that, according to the Gnostics, the true story has been manipulated and misinterpreted over the years. According to the Gnostic gospels, Adam and Eve were not actual historical figures, but representatives of two principles within every human being at the time. Adam was the dramatic embodiment of the mind-body, while Eve stood for the spirit. Before Eve came, Adam was stuck in an illusory material reality, where he was unaware of is true nature. In the 'Hypostasis of the Archons', it says "The rulers took counsel with one another and said, "Come, let us cause a deep sleep to fall upon Adam." And he slept. Now the deep sleep that they "caused to fall upon him" is ignorance." Eve is said to have come to help Adam awaken from his sleep and help him escape the "prison of the body". In the 'Apocryphon of John', it is said that Eve told Adam "'I am the Pronoia of the pure light; I am the thinking of the virginal Spirit, who raised you up to the honoured place. Arise and remember that it is you who hearkened, and follow your root, which is I, the merciful one, and guard yourself against the angels of poverty and the demons of chaos and all those who ensnare you, and beware of the deep sleep and the enclosure of the inside of Hades." Eve is said to have emerged from within the sleepy Adam to save him from poverty and chaos. In 'The Origin of the World', it says "Sophia (the true God) sent Eve as an instructor, in order that she might make Adam, who had no soul, arise... [Eve] had pity upon [Adam], and she said, "Adam! Become alive! Arise upon the earth!" Immediately her word became accomplished fact. For Adam, having arisen, suddenly opened his eyes." So Eve, who represents the true self of Adam, is viewed as the one who inspired Adam to wake up from his sleep. The serpent is described as being similarly inspired by Sophia (the true God) as Eve. The serpent is described as the instructor who taught Adam and Eve about their source, informing them that they were of high and holy origin and not mere slaves of the creator deity of the material world. While this representational story of the awakening of humanity was supposed to have happened several thousand years ago, it seems that we have all returned to this state of deep sleep, of ignorance, unaware of our true nature. This is because we have believed we are our egos. We must transcend the ego if we are to awaken from our sleep and remember who we truly are, just like Adam did.

Topic 13 Exercises

Day 1

Close your eyes and simply observe your thoughts. Visualise each thought as a cloud in your mind. As a cloud of thought comes, be aware of it and then let it float by without dwelling on it. Instead of focusing on the clouds, focus on the blue sky. This blue sky is who you truly are.

Day 2

Today, we will direct our attention away from our thoughts and focus on the feeling of oneness. So, close your eyes and feel your own consciousness. Simply be aware of awareness. If a thought tries to distract you, bring your attention back to your awareness. This awareness, this consciousness, is completely still and silent, and it has no boundaries, and so it is limitless. The more you focus on this consciousness, the more you will feel oneness as this consciousness is the only thing that truly exists. Notice how at peace you are as you do this exercise.

Day 3

Close your eyes and imagine you are at one of those sushi restaurants where the food comes out on a conveyor belt. Visualise each thought you have as a dish on the conveyor belt. You can decide to either take the dish, open it and eat it, or you can be aware of the dish but decide to let it go by without focusing on it. Today, we choose to let the dishes go by without dwelling on them.

Day 4

Today, we will start working on reprogramming your mind. Go about your day today and mentally note down all the times you experienced a negative emotion. At the end of the day, write all these instances down on a piece of paper. Keep this paper for tomorrow's exercise.

Day 5

With yesterday's paper, spend some today to keep asking yourself "Why?" you felt each of those emotions, until you have identified the negative beliefs that caused you to feel each of those emotions. Write those negative beliefs down next to their associated emotions, and keep this paper for tomorrow's exercise.

Day 6

Take yesterday's paper, and for each negative belief you identified, write a positive belief that you wish to have instead. For instance, if you found that you feared death because of the belief that you are your physical body, you may write down a positive belief like "I am an eternal being who cannot die". Then, spend some time in meditation to take all attention of your ego and its thoughts, and repeat all those positive affirmations. Notice how you feel as a result of this exercise.

Day 7

Now that you have identified positive affirmations that you would like ingrained in your mind, go about your day today, and if you catch yourself experiencing a negative thought or emotion, repeat an appropriate positive affirmation until that negative thought or emotion goes away. By doing this regularly, you will find that your positive affirmations gradually become your new set of beliefs.

TOPIC 14 - LIFE AFTER DEATH

Some of the biggest fears people have is the fear of their own death, or the fear of a loved one's death, or the fear of hell, but today we will look to completely remove these fears from within you. All fears are based on an illusion, and so we will discuss the illusions behind each of those fears.

Heaven & Hell

Almost every single religion tells us that there is life after death in some form. Traditional Christians, Muslims and Zoroastrians believe in a heaven or hell afterlife. Buddhists and Hindus believe that souls keep reincarnating in the material world until they reach nirvana or moksha, where they become their true selves and continue their soul journey outside of the dense material world. In *The Law of One*, Ra tell us that all souls go through thousands of lives during third density in order to try to learn the spiritual lessons needed to progress on to fourth density. Similarly, in Sufism (which is a branch of Islam) and Gnosticism (which can be thought of as an earlier branch of Christianity), it is believed that one reincarnates unless they actively seek gnosis or ma'rifa (which is knowledge of the truth) while they are alive, after which they will reunite with God (or their true self). So Buddhists, Hindus, Sufis and Gnostics all believe that one escapes the cycle of birth and death in the material world when they reach a state of consciousness brought about by seeking the truth of oneself and reality. In this way, they do not believe that hell and heaven are actual places. Heaven is viewed as the state of liberation from the material world once one reaches a high enough state of consciousness, and hell is where one remains in the illusion of the material world full of duality and suffering. Could these also be the original definitions of the heaven and hell referred to in Christianity, Islam and Zoroastrianism?

Think about it for a second – would a loving God create you just so that you worship him and follow a strict lifestyle, otherwise he will punish you forever? This doesn't make sense. When you realise that you are part of God, you will understand that God would never eternally punish itself or want to be eternally apart from itself. Nor can it be apart from itself. And when you realise that the whole point of life is to experience and learn, and that there are no mistakes, you will understand that you would never be punished for experiencing or doing anything. Hell as a place is a myth. You are the decision maker for your soul – you are the one who decides whether to reincarnate or not. You are your own judge. The idea of hell or a punishing God comes from the illusory belief in separation between us and God. But as we have learned throughout this course, there is no separation – you and God are one. Each density can be thought of as a grade or year in school. If you do not learn the lessons you need to learn in order to graduate to the next grade, you simply re-do the year out of choice. There is no punishment for re-doing. In this way, eventually, we will all end up in the exact same destination, which is the graduation of the final year, where we 'reunite with God'.

Hell is not a place but a state of consciousness where one identifies with their ego. Heaven is therefore a state of consciousness where one identifies with their true self. We have explained in previous topics how all suffering is caused by the ego and its thoughts. So heaven is a state of consciousness with no suffering, just pure love and bliss. Many might say that some evil people deserve to go to hell, but there is no one who is inherently evil; they can't be. We are all manifestations of love, of oneness, of God. It is one's ego that causes them to do unloving acts, because the ego is so detached from one's true, loving nature. But we have all identified with our egos at some point, so if you judge another person as deserving of eternal punishment, you are also indirectly saying that everyone, including yourself, deserves eternal punishment. Either we all deserve eternal punishment, or none of us do.

Science

What does science have to say about life after death? Well, Einstein famously discovered that, not only is everything in the universe just energy, but also energy cannot be created or destroyed, only transformed. We have also established in previous topics that we are beings of love and light energy, with love being the zero-point energy, or awareness. What's more, we have also found out that our inner light energy, or life force energy, organises matter around it in such a way as to create our physical bodies. Therefore, our life force energy was never created and can never be destroyed. In other words, this life force energy must have always existed, and it will always exist. The reason many people believe they can die is because they identify with their egos, and every ego believes it is the body and the character that it is playing. Both the body and character can die as they are both illusions. However, if we realise that we are not our egos but that we are consciousness and energy, both of which cannot be destroyed, we can remember our true eternal nature.

NDEs & OBEs

Near-death experiences (NDEs) and Out-of-body experiences (OBEs) are gifts that we are given to help us understand life after death. In many near-death experiences, the person's brain and body are completely dead while they have these experiences. Think about it – if the brain and body are dead but awareness continues to exist, doesn't this mean that we are not our bodies or brains? When researching the thousands of accounts of NDEs and OBEs, you will find that people who experience them seem to all say the same thing. Every OBE and NDE are similar in what they experience, but certain specifics are unique to each person's life. For instance, nearly all experiences seem to report how their soul separates from their body and looks down on their body. They all then go through a tunnel towards a bright light, where they are then overcome with love that they have never felt before, and they see beings of light around them. Despite not having a body during these experiences, they are able to be aware of everything around them. Many come back with the understanding that everything is connected and that we are all co-creators. Many come back very spiritual, believing in God and dedicating their life to helping others. Near-death experiencers come back telling us that no one judges us but ourselves, and that they all decided to come back to earth for a specific purpose, usually because their life purpose hasn't been fulfilled yet, or because they know a loved one needs them. They also come out of the experiences not fearing death at all, but actually looking forward to it. To me, when all these thousands of people who don't know each other are saying the same things, and if all these experiences have the same positive effects on the experiencers' lives afterwards, what more proof could we all need?

People having OBEs and NDEs report a sense of having actually left their physical body, but they have full use of their senses, which are often greatly enhanced. They have freedom of movement and a sense of well-being. They can see things that would normally not be visible to them, such as objects on top of cabinets in the operating room, or on the rooftops of nearby buildings, or family members who are not present in the same room as the experiencer's body. They may know the thoughts of those present in the room with them, or report precise details of conversations that occurred when they were under general anaesthesia. Dr Kenneth Ring and Sharon Cooper performed a study examining the NDEs of people who have been blind from birth. The results offer particularly compelling evidence of the existence of consciousness beyond the body, because these people have never been able to see. Unlike sighted people having NDEs who are describing objects and people they have witnessed before, blind people have no such frame of reference. During their NDEs, blind people have been able to describe details of objects they have never seen. One such experiencer was a 45-year-old woman named Vicki Umipeg, whose optic nerve had been destroyed at birth by an overdose of oxygen. She reported "I don't see anything, not even in my dreams, not even black." After a car accident, she was taken to the emergency room. She found her awareness floating above her body: "I found myself in the hospital looking down at what was happening, frightened since I had never 'seen' before". Vicki was disoriented and had difficulty recognising that the body she was staring down at was hers: "I knew that it was mine because I wasn't in mine". Vicki was later able to describe the doctor and nurse who were working on her unconscious body, as well as their words: "They kept saying, 'We can't bring her back.' I felt very detached from my body and couldn't understand why they were upset. I went up through the ceiling hearing beautiful sounds of wind chimes. Where I was I could see trees, birds, and people but all made of light. I was overwhelmed because I couldn't imagine what light was like. It was like a place where all knowledge was. I was then sent back and into my body in excruciating pain." Vicki was also able to describe details of objects she had never been able to see, such as the patterns on her rings: "I think I was wearing the plain gold band on my right ring finger and my father's wedding ring next to it. But my wedding ring I definitely saw... That was the one I noticed the most because it's most unusual. It has orange blossoms on the corners of it." Vicki later said that this experience was "the only time I could ever relate to seeing and to what light was, because I experienced it."

Past Lives

History is full of remarkable discoveries of individuals who had factual knowledge of people who lived before them in places they had never been. Perhaps one of the most convincing cases of a past life reality is the story of James Leninger published in a book, Soul Survivor, which was written by his parents. Three weeks after James Leninger's second birthday, he began to experience the same terrifying nightmare, night after night. In his sleep, James would shout out recurring phrases such as "Plane on fire! Little man can't get out!" Out of concern for their son's welfare, Bruce and Andrea Leninger pieced together what their son was communicating and eventually discovered that he was reliving the past life of World War II fighter pilot James Huston. Huston was stationed on the aircraft carrier U.S.S Natoma Bay and died after being shot down in a battle over the Sea of Japan. When young James was taken to a reunion of Natoma Bay veterans, he recognised many by name. When the Leningers found out that one of James Huston's siblings was still alive, they contacted her. Through their conversations, James was able to accurately recall Huston's family history that he experienced while in his former life as James Huston. Soul Survivor is a riveting true story of how the Leningers' belief system, which did not include a belief in reincarnation, was shaken to the core, as they came to recognise the fact that their little boy, against all odds and in the face of true sceptics, including themselves, nevertheless harboured the soul of a man who died long ago.

Dolores Cannon was a lovely woman who developed a hypnosis technique that allowed her to take her patients through past life regressions. These past life regressions helped her patients heal certain diseases and identify what karmic ties they had with previous lives. She took her patients through the death process and beyond in order to discover what happens after death. After doing this with thousands of patients, she said they all said the same things about what happens after death:

1) They feel very cold and they instantly leave the body and are looking down on their body

2) They then go through a tunnel towards a bright light

3) Near-death experiencers are encouraged to go back and never get beyond the light, and usually they do decide to go back because they realise a loved one needs them, but it is completely their decision. However, for those who die, they go through the light, which is described as a huge energy source, which some have called God.

4) The silver cord is then shattered. Everyone is connected to the spirit realm with a silver cord. Once it is shattered, you cannot return back to that body again. This is similar to what the spiritual teacher Osho said in his The Book of Secrets – he said that within our spine, there is an invisible thread-like silver cord of energy. Our spines are connected to our whole body, and so Osho says that the cord is our life. It's what connects our visible and invisible existence. It is through this thread that we are connected to our soul.

5) There are three different astral planes you can then go to, depending on your vibration. These astral planes are places where souls can heal from trauma and negativity, review their lives, and decide when and where to reincarnate again. They may reincarnate based on wanting to repay some karma, to learn new spiritual lessons or help other souls learn lessons, or to have certain experiences before they progress. The astral planes are also where souls can learn spiritual principles, but the schools in these planes are described as book learning, while incarnating in a physical body is like hands-on experience. According to Ra in The Law of One, third density is where most of the soul's learning occurs, and where the most

enriching experiences are, so many of us are keen to re-incarnate several times to gain as much knowledge and experience as we can. Therefore, reincarnation is completely our choice.

Dolores' patients taught her that life is just all a play, a game. The souls also told her that everything is inter-woven because we are all one and we are all everything. Whatever we do, say or think affects everyone. They also taught her that nobody dies until they're ready to die, and everyone chooses how they are going to die. Dolores says that she has never had someone describe an after-death experience as bad or negative. She has written many books about the details of certain people's past lives that are notable. These books have incredible detail in them that have later been proven as accurate; details that one could not have known from research.

Dr Ian Stevenson has researched thousands of cases of young children remembering their past lives. He would note down what a child was saying about their past life, and then he did some research to try and find the person who matched the description the child gave him. He would use information such as how the person died, where they lived, information about relationships with others, birth defects, phobias and allergies. In many cases, Dr Stevenson found a match of the life the child remembers, and he would then find people who were close to the person from the previous life and ask them to confirm the details. He would also often confirm details of the way the children claimed they died with police reports and autopsies. From his findings, we can conclude that there is a very strong scientific case for reincarnation.

Mediums

A medium connects with someone's loved ones in spirit, and gives enough detailed evidence to demonstrate that they're really linking with a specific individual. While, yes, there may be some mediums who might give very vague information, there are many mediums who give such specific information that there could be no possible way of them knowing it other than genuinely communicating with the dead. The intention of mediumship is to let someone know that their deceased loves ones are still a part of their lives, provide closure and bereavement support, and diminish the fear of death. Loved ones in spirit may offer messages of love, support, and healing, or specific information understood only by the sitter. If you are curious, I encourage you to find a highly-rated medium near you and try it out for yourself. How can these mediums do their jobs unless souls never truly die, and they continue to live on after the physical death?

The Fear of Someone Else's Death

Why do people fear someone else's death? One of the main reasons is the fear of being alone. But you must realise that you can choose to view yourself as always alone, or you can choose to see that you are never alone. You are always alone in the sense that your consciousness is the only consciousness that has ever existed, and the different beings and characters are just illusions. Or you can choose to see that you are never alone, because you are always energetically connected to all beings in the universe, whether they are physically alive or not, no matter how much physical distance there is between you. Remember, distance and death are illusions, and in reality, all is connected in oneness. Therefore, you cannot just be alone some of the time. When you come to know this fully, you will no longer fear being alone.

When a loved one dies, people are often depressed because they feel that the person should have lived for longer, or the death shouldn't have happened. But when you realise that each soul chooses how and when they die, you realise there was no mistake; the soul felt it was time to leave. It is the ego that resists life, thinking it should go a certain way. So when someone dies, there is of course the initial shock, but it is then the ego that feels depressed and doesn't feel like life should have gone this way. It is also the ego that lives in the past and will use someone's death as a way to romanticise the past and deem the present moment unsatisfactory in comparison. Your true self never weeps and never resists life. You can either choose to listen to the ego's thoughts that will keep you in suffering for a long time after a person's death, or you can decide to appreciate the good times you had with that person, be grateful for the lessons you learned from your relationship and experiences with that person, and move on by living in the present. Grieving and feeling depressed and angry after someone's death is the result of a choice one makes to listen to their ego's thoughts.

We get so attached to people's illusory characters and bodies, because that's who we choose to believe people are. Since illusions eventually change or die, our attachments eventually cause us suffering. This is why people feel grief when someone dies; they feel there has been a loss. However, if we were instead to view each other as eternal souls, then we don't ever have to feel sad when someone's physical body dies because we would know that the person's true self lives on, and that the person had simply completed what they came to do in that particular earthly life. Ultimately, you are everyone and everything. You are always surrounded by yourself in different forms. Forms come and go, but the underlying essence of you is always there.

Light body

Thousands of Tibetan Buddhist monks transform into what's called a "rainbow body" when they die. The Institute of Noetic Sciences has documented 160,000 of such cases. In most cases, the physical body would shrink to a child-sized body, and a light can be seen to ascend from the body. In other cases, the body completely vanishes. Weeks before the transformation, some can engrave their hand or foot into a cave wall. The monks say that the secret to this is to only have loving thoughts for 13 – 60 years. When you align more with your true, loving self, your inner light (or life force energy) shines more brightly. Therefore, it makes sense that if we only have loving thoughts for many years, the light within us would be so strong that it can actually be seen leaving the body upon physical death. The 'physical' body somewhat hides our inner light, and so, once the physical body is shed, one's inner light can be more easily seen. The fact that the light bodies of these monks have actually been seen leaving their bodies when they die further supports the case that we are all eternal beings, and that once we finish what we came to do in a particular life, our true selves live on.

Different Points Within Soul Journeys

Why do you think some people are just naturally more wise, loving, forgiving or compassionate than others? You may have felt quite different to most others throughout your life, and may have felt like the odd one out all the time – why do you think that is? Why are some people optimists and more positive, while others are pessimists and have a more negative attitude towards everything? Why do some people look to find the joy in everything, while others always look to find what's wrong with life? Why do some people learn life lessons a lot more quickly than others? Why are some people so selfish and self-centred, but others are extremely selfless? Why are some people so focused on spirituality, yet others are atheists and don't want anything to do with spirituality? I am not talking about differences in personality here, but the differences between us in terms of states of consciousness. If we all just live once, then what could possibly explain these huge differences in levels of consciousness we see on Earth?

It can only be explained by reincarnation. Some people have reincarnated more than others, and so are further along on their spiritual path. The more life experience you have, the more likely you are to be more spiritually developed, and so the likelier you are to have a higher state of consciousness. And the higher your state of consciousness, the more joyous, loving, peaceful, compassionate, selfless and forgiving you are, and the more likely you are to be an optimist, have a positive attitude about things, learn life lessons quickly, and the more likely you are to be interested in actively exploring spirituality. It is the only explanation.

Again, to address any issue, it is important that we transcend the material world to find the truth. If you cannot see beyond the material world, then you will not believe that you are an eternal being, because all you can see with your physical eyes is that people die and that's it. This is the 'hell' state of consciousness that is full of suffering. However, if you are more willing to explore beyond the physical, material world, you allow yourself to eventually discover the truth; that we are all just one eternal consciousness. This is the 'heaven' state of consciousness, where you will be free from all suffering. At the root of all suffering is fear, and this fear is the result of believing in separation. When one forgets their true, eternal nature, their biggest fear is the fear of death. The fear of death is based on the belief that you are your physical body, and so, when you come to fully remember that you cannot die because you are not your physical body, you will no longer fear death. If you still fear death, just ask yourself this - is your belief that your physical death will be the end of you something that you have come to know from within yourself, or is it what you have been taught to believe by outside sources?

Topic 14 Exercises

Day 1

Close your eyes today and feel like your body is peeling, shedding or dissolving away. What is left is a bright white light. Just be this bright light for a few minutes. Feel how this light is eternal, and will continue to exist forever.

Day 2

I want you to think about the people you were close to who have now died. If you feel grief or sadness, ask yourself why. Why do you feel sad? They came here to fulfil a purpose and they did, so why do you feel sad? When we bring awareness to our emotions, we can see the illusions behind them.

Day 3

Today, I would like you to research some accounts of near-death experiences. There are many accounts on Youtube. What do they say about death? Does this eliminate your fears around death? How do you feel when they give their accounts?

Day 4

Close your eyes and sit with the knowledge that you have lived many hundreds, perhaps thousands, of lives. Sit with the knowledge that you can never truly die. What a relief this is. Isn't it fascinating? After doing this for a few minutes, see how you feel now about your body eventually dying. Do you still fear your own death?

Day 5

Take some time today to close your eyes and go beyond your thoughts. Your thoughts are associated with the material world, and so if you transcend your thoughts, you can transcend the material world. Behind all these thoughts is your still, silent consciousness. Your thoughts usually distract you from experiencing this consciousness, but they are just on the surface. Go beyond the surface today to see the truth of your consciousness. Really feel how this consciousness is eternal.

Day 6

Let's look at some more accounts of near-death experiences today. Notice how you feel as you hear these accounts. Is your heart telling you that what they are saying is true?

Day 7

Take some time today to think about how your body and character will eventually die. Really come to terms with this fact. Notice any negative thoughts and emotions that arise when contemplating this. Become aware of these thoughts and emotions, and in so doing, they will dissolve away.

TOPIC 15 - LIFE'S SIMPLE CHOICE

Life becomes so simple when you spiritually awaken and become more aware of everything. There is a simple choice you can choose to make in every moment of your life – love or fear. Even if there seem to be more options to choose from, all those options can be broadly categorised into either love or fear.

Let me start by asking you what is fear? What causes fear? Like any emotion, fear is the body's energetic response to certain thoughts. So what thoughts lead to fear? Why do we have those thoughts? Do we choose to think of those thoughts or do they just pop up in our minds without our control? Of course, no one chooses to feel fear. Thoughts that lead to fear arise subconsciously without our conscious control. Initially, many might say that it is the spider that causes them to fear, or looking down from a skyscraper, or being diagnosed with a health condition, or suddenly having a financial disaster. In this way, many people believe that the cause of their fear is external to them. But as we have learned in previous topics, it is the ego's response to our external environment that causes our suffering, not the external environment itself. The cause of our fear must therefore be within us, just like any other emotion. It is our thoughts of worst-case scenarios that lead to emotions of fear. These thoughts are automatic reactions of the subconscious mind to our external environment. So the input to our mind is the information gained from our senses about the external environment, and the outputs of the mind are the thoughts of worst-case scenarios. And what changes the inputs of our mind into the outputs? It is our programmed beliefs.

Our programmed beliefs are what actually cause our fears, not the external environment. The spider is not what causes your fear, but it's your programmed beliefs about what the spider may do to you. It is not looking down from a skyscraper that causes your fear, but it's your programmed belief that you may fall from the height. It is not the health condition that causes your fear, but it's your programmed beliefs about how this will affect the life you envisioned for yourself. It is not the huge financial disaster that causes your fear, but it's your programmed belief that you need that money to survive. But where do these beliefs come from? Are they really your beliefs? Again, it's the same culprit – the ego. The ego's beliefs are based on our upbringing, education, society, culture, media programming, and other past experiences. It has these beliefs because these are what it has been taught, or what it has experienced in the past.

Notice how every fear is the thought of something undesirable happening in the future. When you are at a height from the ground, you are not scared of currently being on top of a skyscraper, but you're scared of potentially falling from the skyscraper. You are not scared of being next to a spider, you're scared of the spider perhaps poisoning you in the near future. You are not scared of the diagnosis of the health condition, you're scared of how it may affect your future. You're not scared because of the big bill you get in the post, but you're scared of perhaps not being able to survive in the future as a result of the bill. So every fear is the fear of the future, not the present. Therefore, we have established that all fear is fear of the future based on past experiences. Fear cannot exist while being completely present. When living in the present, the thoughts of worst-case scenarios may still arise in you, but you choose not to listen to them. In this way, you have detached from the ego's thoughts and have not allowed the thoughts to lead to emotions of fear. You can then turn your attention away from your ego's thoughts and towards your environment.

Being present is not the only way to overcome fear though. Every fear has at its very core the fear of death. As we learned in the previous topic, one only fears death because they have forgotten their true eternal self. They have believed that they are separate from the world around them. Therefore, dropping all programmed beliefs and remembering who you truly is actually the best way to permanently eliminate all fears. And the best way to remember who you truly are is disassociate and detach from your ego during meditations. By becoming aware of your ego, you become awareness. Only awareness can be aware of the ego. The ego cannot be aware of itself because it is not real; it is a figment of your mind's imagination. It is not a real being. So whenever you are aware of anything, not just your ego, then you know that you are aligning with your true self.

When you get fear out of the way, you are automatically loving. True love is not an effort, it is who you truly are.

By getting the ego out of the Divine's way, you get fear out of love's way. Love and fear are the two opposite energies that can be expressed through you. By living in fear, you choose not to love, and by living as love, you choose not to fear. Love is therefore the antidote to fear. When you love yourself, how can you feel guilt or jealousy? When you love others, how can you feel anger? When you love life, how can you feel anxious or depressed? Loving yourself, loving others, and loving life is automatic when you disassociate from your ego. The ego's thoughts will always lead to fear as the ego is a set of beliefs that are based on the illusion of separation, and the belief in separation is what causes all fears. However, when you disassociate from your ego, you will remember the oneness of all life, and you will be in a constant state of love, peace, joy and bliss as a result.

When you choose love, you learn to live from your heart. Instead of following your ego, which always guides you based on what it thinks you should be doing or what others expect you to do, you follow your heart, which always guides you based on what will bring you joy. Most people follow their ego's guidance out of fear; they think that if they do what they should be doing or what they are expected to do, they will gain acceptance from others. It is the fear of not being accepted and loved by others that motivates people to follow their ego's guidance rather than their heart. For instance, many people do not pursue their dream career because they are scared that they will not be successful in the eyes of others. Many people do not express their true feelings to others because they are scared of how others will react. Many people do not end their toxic relationships because they are scared of being alone. But the only reason people fear not being accepted or loved by others is because they don't love or accept themselves. And people do not love and accept themselves because they believe they are their imperfect, illusory egos and have forgotten who they truly are. As we have previously discussed, when one remembers who they truly are, loving themselves, loving others and loving life will be automatic because they will have realised that all is love and all is one. It is often easier to follow the path of fear as fear is such an intense motivator, while love is a more gentle and peaceful guide. One must distance themselves from the loudness of fear to be able to hear the voice of love. When one chooses love instead, they simply do what brings them joy. Because they have found that inner love, they do not need the acceptance and love from others, which gives them the freedom to follow their joy. Every decision you need to make in life is based on these two choices – do you choose love by following your heart, or do you choose fear by following your ego?

People are scared to choose love because they feel it makes them vulnerable. They feel vulnerable because choosing love means choosing uncertainty. When you choose to be in the present moment, you become vulnerable to what the present moment brings. When you choose to love someone, you open yourself up to them and become vulnerable to them. When you choose to pursue your dream career, you become vulnerable to how others will respond to the services you offer. When you choose to follow your heart, you become vulnerable to whatever that leads to. By choosing love, you release all attachments and expectations, and your ego surrenders control of your life to the Divine within you. Your ego hates stepping into the world of uncertainty and the unknown because, to the ego, this is a dangerous way of living. It prefers a much more predictable life because it fears death, so if it can know its safety and comfort is more guaranteed, it will be happier. However, uncertainty is where the beauty, surprises, laughter and magic of life lies. When you open yourself up to uncertainty, your life will be full of joy and love. How can life miraculously surprise you if you never give it a chance by being vulnerable to it? Yes, there may be challenging times, but when you follow your heart, you will always be able to hear the inner guidance that will help you overcome those challenges. If, out of fear, you choose to follow what is safe, your life will become boring, predictable, and devoid of love. It's time to make the conscious choice of uncertainty rather than predictability, enjoyment rather than boredom, freedom rather than being programmed, following your heart rather than following your mind, the Divine rather than ego, surrender rather than control, truth rather than illusion. In other words, it's time to choose love rather than fear. You are given free will to make this choice at any moment. You have experienced a life based on fear up until now - if you are not happy with how your life is going, why not choose love instead and see how it goes? I promise that you will not regret it.

Topic 15 Exercises

<u>Day 1</u>

Notice your inner state as you go about your day today and keep evaluating whether you are in a state of love or fear. If you have been engaging with the ego's thoughts, you are likely to be in a state of fear. If you are present with your surroundings, then you will be in a state of love. At the end of the day, estimate what percentage of the day you spent in love. Are you surprised by the result?

Day 2

At the end of the day, identify every single decision you made today, no matter how insignificant you believe those decisions are. Each of those decisions were either done in love or fear, without exception. Now identify whether each decision was based on love or based on fear. Are you surprised by the result?

Day 3

Before you make any decision today, any decision at all, no matter how small, remind yourself that the choice is between love and fear. You can feel in your heart what the love option is. The mind is responsible for decisions made out of fear. If you want to choose love, go with what excites you rather than what your mind says makes sense.

Day 4

Throughout your day today, keep asking yourself the following question: "Am I in love or am I in fear?" Notice how the awareness of these two choices affects the decisions you make today. Did you change your behaviour to follow the path of love?

Day 5

Make some time today to review the major decisions you have made in your life. Were they done out of love, or were they done out of fear? Do you regret making any of the decisions based on love? Did you regret the decisions based on fear? If you go through life following a safe and predictable path based on fear, you will be riddled with regret and feelings of "What if?" However, if you go through life following your heart, there cannot be regrets. Yes, you may experience tough challenges, but each challenge is an opportunity to learn something.

Day 6

What are your current fears? Note them all down. As we have learned so far in this course, all fears, without exception, are based on some form of illusion. Next to each fear you have identified, note down what illusory beliefs are behind this fear. Then, next to each illusory belief, write the affirmation "I choose love instead".

Day 7

Today, every moment will be spent in love. This means not listening to the ego's thoughts. It means only doing what brings you joy. It means being completely present with what life brings you today. It means expressing exactly what you want to say rather than people-pleasing all the time. How did this affect your day? Did it lead to positive outcomes or negative outcomes? Did you enjoy your day more?

TOPIC 16 - WHAT THE HELL ARE CHAKRAS?

You might have heard the word 'chakra' being thrown about before when learning about spirituality, or when doing practices like yoga, or whenever you meet a hippie. But what the hell are chakras? And why is it important to know about them?

We discussed in previous topics about how we each have an inner light, which is our life force energy. This light is is the source of our body's electromagnetic field. We looked at the scientific evidence proving how this light is received and stored by our DNA, and is then converted into frequencies of energies that are used by our bodies for many different biological processes. The life force energy is transported to all cells, tissues, muscles and organs of the body through what's known as meridian pathways. The ends of these meridian pathways are what's known as acupuncture points on our skin. Our life force energy has seven main energetic centres within the body, and each energy centre is known as a chakra. There are other chakras outside the body, but we will tackle the basic seven within the body in this level of the course.

These centres are along the spine of the body, and are where the body's meridian pathways lead from.

Each centre is responsible for circulating different frequencies of energies around the body, and different frequencies of energy are needed for different biological processes. Remember how we explained that emotions are the body's energetic responses to thoughts? The physical manifestation of these energetic responses are in the form of hormones, and each chakra corresponds with a major hormonal gland within the body. Therefore, the energy of a chakra is linked to the secretion of hormones from its associated hormonal gland.

The seven chakras correspond exactly with the seven colours of the rainbow – from violet to red. The energy of the violet chakra has the highest frequency and the energies of the red chakra has the lowest frequency, just as ultraviolet light has the highest frequency within the visible light spectrum, and infra-red light has the lowest. So when I say that you are a being of light, I mean it literally – you have a rainbow of energies within you. Our inner light first enters the body through the lowest chakra and then moves its way up to the highest chakra. All health problems occur when our inner light is unable to flow properly to all areas of the body. This is usually caused by either a blockage or overactivity in one or more chakras. When a chakra is overactive, too much light energy is being used by that chakra, which does not leave enough energy to be used by higher chakras. When there is a blockage in a chakra, this means that light is being prevented from travelling to the chakra's corresponding areas of the body, and light is also being inhibited from rising up to be used by the higher chakras and their corresponding areas of the body.

We will now go through each chakra to find out the corresponding hormonal gland and what emotions they are responsible for. We will then also discover the symptoms of overactivity or blockages in each chakra. Let's work from the bottom up:

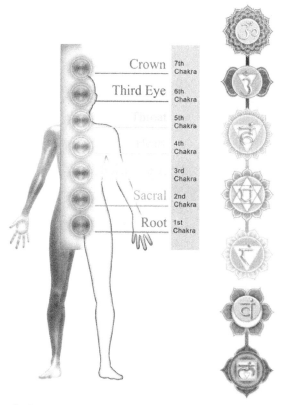

1) Root Chakra

Colour: Red.

Location: At the coccyx.

Associated Glands & Hormones: Digestive glands which

are responsible for digestive enzymes, and the adrenal glands which secrete hormones like adrenaline, which stimulates the 'fight or flight' response.

Function: This chakra is all about survival consciousness. It has to do with consumption, digestion, elimination, and the breaking down of food into energy. It is also related to social networks and structures, relationships, support systems, and family cultures.

Balanced When: You feel grounded, safe, and secure. When you are eating right and sleeping well. When you are fearless and believe that you will always have what you need to survive. Also, if you have a good support network around you from family and friends then your root chakra will likely be balanced.

Blocked When: You are afraid of how you can survive – for instance, if you are having financial problems, experiencing instability, you feel physically threatened, or whenever you are feeling anxiety or fear. Basically, if you feel you are lacking something you need then your root chakra will be blocked. This includes support from family and friends. When one's root chakra is blocked, they are in survival mode.

Overactive When: One overeats, or when one is materialistic, greedy, aggressive, or competitive.

2) Sacral Chakra

Colour: Orange

Location: Lower abdomen

Associated Glands & Hormones: Sexual glands responsible for oestrogen, progesterone and testosterone.

Function: Connection to others through sex and intimacy. Passion, creativity, optimism, sensual pleasure.

Balanced When: One has a healthy sexual relationship with someone, and/or when one is able to freely express their creativity. If someone is following their passions, this is another sign of a balanced sacral chakra.

Blocked When: One feels disconnected from others, has sexual problems, a lack of desire, jealousy, addiction problems, need for approval, feelings of shame or guilt, no creativity, lack of intimacy, or trauma from molestation.

Overactive When: One is a sex addict, or is manipulative in a sexual relationship.

3) Solar Plexus Chakra

Colour: Yellow

Location: Upper abdomen

Associated Glands & Hormones: Adrenal & pancreatic glands associated with adrenaline, cortisol, kidney hormones, liver and stomach enzymes, and insulin.

Function: Feelings of control, self-esteem, willpower, assertiveness, aggression, dominance, trust in one's self.

Balanced When: One has drive, confidence, and a sense of direction in life. When one uses will to overcome their environment and conditions.

Blocked When: One feels a lack of purpose, has low self-esteem, feels powerless, has motivation issues, or if one feels the world is against them and they have no control over their life. It can also be blocked in someone who is submissive, or in someone who allows others to control or influence them.

Overactive When: One is very controlling, overpowering,

thoughtless, power hungry, critical, judgemental, or manipulative to get what they want. It can also be overactive in someone who is very angry, defensive or aggressive.

4) Heart Chakra

Colour: Green

Location: Centre of Chest

Associated Glands & Hormones: Thymus gland responsible for growth hormone, oxytocin and many chemicals that stimulate the immune system's health.

Function: Love, compassion and forgiveness of one's self and others.

Balanced When: One is caring, kind, patient, trusting, grateful, appreciative, or selfless. When one feels connected to everything and everyone around them, and sees beauty in all things. When one loves themselves.

Blocked When: Feeling lonely, paranoid, bitter, or hateful. It is also blocked when someone has trust issues, a lack of compassion or empathy, or is generally not great at relationships with others. When one feels guilt or shame and is too hard on themselves.

Overactive When: Someone is very self-sacrificing, co-dependent, over-promising, or jealous. When one loves others more than themselves, or loves themselves more than they love others.

5) Throat Chakra

Colour: Blue

Location: Top of the throat

Associated Glands & Hormones: Thyroid and salivary glands associated with thyroid hormones and parathyroid chemicals.

Function: Communication of one's truth. Wisdom. Speaking and listening. Expression of one's self.

Balanced When: One is able to effectively communicate how they feel. When one is a good listener. When one is able to express their love towards others.

Blocked When: You feel you are misunderstood, or when you feel you are unable to truly express yourself properly. Also, when one doesn't listen to others, or when they are holding a lot of secrets.

Overactive When: One talks excessively or is very argumentative. When one is opinionated, gossipy, loud, talking over others, or uses a lot of curse words.

6) Third Eye Chakra

Colour: Indigo

Location: Middle of the brain in line with the gap between your eyebrows

Associated Glands & Hormones: Pineal gland which secretes serotonin and melatonin.

Function: Creativity, visualisation, imagination, memory & focus, extra-sensory abilities.

Balanced When: One is able to manifest things in their life or use their extrasensory abilities. When one tunes in with divine intelligence and their intuition. When one can see past material illusions.

Blocked When: One doesn't believe in anything other than what they can sense, or when one has a busy mind, weak concentration, non-stop thinking, insomnia, ADD, or memory problems.

Overactive When: Someone takes a lot of psychedelic drugs, which may create many hallucinations or hysteria. In these cases, one can perceive the spiritual realm but is not grounded and can't integrate their perception into 'normal' life, so they'll seem really crazy to others.

7) Crown chakra

Colour: Violet

Location: Top of the head

Associated Glands & Hormones: Pituitary gland, which is known as the master gland because it governs and creates harmony with all the other glands.

Function: This connects you to your higher self.

Balanced When: Someone has remembered oneness and is in harmony with all things. When someone has total inner peace and bliss.

Blocked When: One believes in separation, or when someone is so disconnected from spirituality, or when someone fears the unknown. This can lead to destructive behaviour and depression. Basically, when your actions reflect a belief that you are separate from God.

Energy Sources

If our inner light energy is being constantly used by the body, would this light energy run out? The answer is no, because we are constantly replenishing this light energy. This light energy is a lower-dimensional form of consciousness; it is a gift from God. Every human receives these gifts of light through each breath, through the food they eat, and by exposing their skin to the sun. As we partake in any of those three activities, our bodies absorb light, and this light is first directed to our root chakra, and then it works its way upwards, being used by all our chakras. Different chakras send different frequencies of light to different areas of the body. However, there is another main way one can receive light which is not used by every human. One opens themselves up to receive more high-frequency light by going within and exploring who they really are. When one seeks knowledge of the self and the Creator, and therefore starts to spiritually awaken, they open themselves up to divine high-frequency energy, which spirals downwards from their crown chakra.

Both inputs of energy converge at a certain chakra, or energy centre, depending on the being's state of consciousness. As Ra says, "The measure of an entity's level of ray activity is the locus wherein the south pole outer energy has been met by the inner spiralling positive energy. As an entity grows more polarized, this locus will move upwards.". So for a third density being, the meeting of the two energies will primarily be at the solar plexus chakra. For a fifth density being, the two energies will primarily meet at the throat chakra. As third density beings, we are born with our first three chakras fully activated, while we have the potential to activate the rest. A second density being, like an animal, will only have the first two chakras fully activated. As we spiritually progress, we activate more chakras, and so the convergence locus rises. We have discussed how the spiritual journey is a journey of self-discovery; the more you remember about who you truly are, the more chakras you activate. In third density, our aim is to activate the upper chakras, starting with the heart chakra (the fourth chakra).

This activation must come from seeking within for knowledge of the self and the Creator, but this inner seeking can be initiated by other beings. For instance, when love is given from someone to a third density being, this love is a higher vibration energy that comes from the fourth chakra, the heart chakra. This love then initiates the third density being to start realising that they are a being who is loveable, thereby allowing them to know more about their true self. As the third density being feels love within themselves, they begin to give love to others, and so they start activating their heart chakra. Another example is when someone who is spiritually advanced communicates their truth to others. They are sending energy through their throat chakra - their fifth energy centre. These words of wisdom encourage others to know more about who they truly are, which can drive them to go within and activate their upper chakras. Another common example is when we see people using their extrasensory abilities, perhaps when we meet a medium or a psychic, or perhaps when we hear an inspiring story of how someone has consciously manifested something that they wanted to experience. They are using their third eye chakra to do these things. This usually astonishes us and makes us question, "How do they do this? If they can do it, surely so can I". We can then begin to seek within for the knowledge of truth, thereby activating our higher chakras. Ra also explain that this is how second density beings, like animals, progress to third density; when we have pets, we show animals love from our heart chakra, thereby encouraging them to raise their vibration.

There is a science to all this; it is based on the physics principle of entrainment. This principle states that when an energy with a certain frequency is surrounded by energies that vibrate at a higher frequency, the energy with the lower frequency gradually increases its vibration to match that of the higher frequency energies. Therefore, if only your first three chakras are activated, when you are surrounded by love from others, you are encouraged to raise your vibration to match this love. This is why when we are around people who have positive attitudes towards life, this positivity rubs off on us. When we are around people who are motivated, we become more motivated. When we are around people who are kind and loving, we find ourselves being more kind and loving. This is why it is so important to only surround yourself with high-vibrational people if you want to raise your vibration. This is also broadly how energy healing or spiritual healing works – the practitioner is able to call upon divine high-vibrational energy, which they allow to flow through their body, and they direct this energy towards their hands. The practitioner then surrounds the part of the patient's body that requires attention with their hands, and this high-vibrational energy raises the vibration of that part of the patient until the patient is healed.

Transforming Energy

On our spiritual journey, we are encouraged to increase our vibration until we become one with God, the highest vibration. As we know more about our true selves, we increase our vibration and activate more of the higher chakras. However, even though we are consistently encouraged to progress through the chakras, those who experience any blockages or overactivity in the first three chakras will find it difficult to activate their upper chakras. For instance, if one is constantly worried about their survival, their root chakra will be blocked, which means they are unlikely to be able to give and receive love (as this occurs through the fourth chakra). Or if someone is obsessed with material gains, power and status, they are unlikely to be able to see past material illusions, which occurs in the third eye chakra, because their solar plexus chakra is overactive. Therefore, to activate higher chakras, one must first work on unblocking and balancing their lower three chakras. Suppressed emotions are what cause chakra blockages. For instance, when you do not appropriately process your emotions relating to a previous sexual abuse, you block your sacral chakra. And if you have suppressed a lot of fear, your root chakra will likely be blocked. Therefore, by appropriately dealing with your suppressed emotions (by the methods we discussed in topic 10), and not suppressing any emotions going forward, you can ensure your lower three chakras are unblocked. When a chakra is overactive, too much energy is being projected outwards, and so, again, there is not enough life force energy left to rise and activate the upper chakras. Both suppression and projection, which cause chakra blockages and overactivity respectively, are subconsciously done by a mind that believes in the illusions of separation. Once you remember the truth of oneness, then you no longer experience negative emotions, and therefore you will no longer need to suppress or project anything. Remember, you are not a victim to life; you are only a victim to the illusory programmed beliefs that you hold so dear.

Until you remember the truth of oneness, the best thing to do when you experience negative emotions is to actually transform that low-vibrational energy into high-vibrational energy which can then be used by your higher chakras. So when an emotion is created by one of your chakras, instead of projecting it outwards and causing an overactivity in that chakra, and instead of resisting and suppressing that emotion which causes a blockage in that chakra, you can become aware of the emotion and feel it fully as discussed in topic 10. By doing this, you allow that energy to rise higher up the chakra system and be used for positive purposes. For instance, if someone is worried about their survival, instead of just suppressing their emotions of fear, they can transform that energy into creating a direction for their life to overcome the challenging situation they are experiencing. Another example is if you have sexual energy arise in you; instead of just releasing it through ejaculation, you can transform that energy into doing something loving for someone. The important thing to note is that there is no such thing as bad energy. Energy is just energy - it's neutral. What that energy manifests as is up to us. So, whatever energy arises in you, don't judge that energy, but just accept that this has arisen in you. You can then decide what to use that energy for; you can suppress that energy, you could project that energy outward at someone or something, or you can transform it into something else within. In truth, with practice and discipline, you can transform any energy into any other type of energy. You can transform sexual energy into energies that can be used to help you manifest what you want. You can even transform hatred into love.

Ra in *The Law of One* state that the goal is to be perfectly balanced in each chakra. This means that, ideally, you don't have any chakra that is more active or more blocked than the other chakras. Your personal energy should be equally balanced among the chakras, with all shining brightly and fully. The crown chakra is described as the sum total of the vibratory level of the individual, and so it can't itself be balanced. Therefore, one must look to balance the other six chakras. To be balanced, one needs to ensure that there are no blockages or overactivity in any chakra, and one needs to continuously seek more knowledge about themselves in order to ensure all chakras are activated. Once a being has fully activated and balanced all their chakras, they can see the true reality of all things and have full knowledge of their true divinity. They fully remember their oneness with God – this is enlightenment.

Topic 16 Exercises

<u>Day 1</u>

At the end of the day, review your day to identify any negative emotions that arose within you, no matter how small or insignificant you think they were. Now think about what happened to each of these energies – did you suppress them, did you project them outwards, or did you take the time to transform these energies into higher-vibrational energy?

<u>Day 2</u>

Whenever you feel any emotional energies arise in you today, take some time to decide what you want to do with those energies. The aim is to be constantly aware of the energies and vibrations within you, so that you can then consciously decide what you want to use those energies for. Without becoming conscious of energies like this, your ego will react automatically to your experiences, often suppressing emotions or projecting them on to others. You could decide that you want to use certain energies to show love, or to help you freely express how you feel, or to help with manifestation. Just state to yourself what you want to use that energy for - this will be enough for today.

Day 3

At the end of the day today, remind yourself what the strongest negative emotion you felt today was. In your mind, replay the experience that triggered this negative emotion. Now, notice the ego's reaction to this experience and the resulting emotional energy. Does it try to blame anything or anyone outside of you for this negative emotion? Does it want to avoid feeling this negative emotion?

Day 4

At the end of the day today, remind yourself what the strongest negative emotion you felt today was. In your mind, replay the experience that triggered this negative emotion. Now, unlike yesterday's exercise, you are going to allow yourself to feel this emotion until it feels like it has dissolved away. The key is not to blame anything or anyone for this energy, but to simply feel it. How do you feel as a result? Do you feel lighter? Do you feel happier? This energy has not actually disappeared, as energy can't just disappear. You have transformed this emotional energy by simply not suppressing it, and by not projecting it outwards.

Day 5

At the end of the day today, take some time to review the

emotions you felt today, and transform them in the same way as you did yesterday. Now, for each emotion, identify what negative beliefs are at the root of that emotion.

Day 6

Take some time today to close your eyes and sit upright. Let's now get to know your three lower chakras. Start from your root chakra - just focus on that chakra until you can easily feel it within you. Once you actually feel the energy of that chakra within you, move up to the next chakra and do the same. Keep doing this until you have clearly felt each of the lower three chakras within you. Don't worry if it takes a while, just keep persevering. They should feel like balls of energy.

Day 7

Today, we will repeat yesterday's exercise, but this time we will get to know the four higher chakras. Start with the heart chakra, focus on it until you can feel it within you, and then move up to the next chakra. The hardest part of this exercise is to maintain focus on a chakra without getting distracted with thoughts. The more you practice this exercise, the easier you will find it.

TOPIC 17 - DIET, HEALTH & SPIRITUALITY

In this topic, we are going to talk about diet and health, and how they relate to spirituality. It's one of my favourite topics. You might ask, "What has diet and health got to do with spirituality?". Well, you are a mind/body/spirit complex - your mind, body and spirit are all connected. Spirituality is all about taking care of your total wellbeing – that includes spiritually, physically and mentally. Your mind is the tool you use to create your reality, your body is the tool that you use to experience your created reality, and you use your experiences to grow spiritually. Therefore, it is essential to take care of your physical body so that you can effectively use this tool for your spiritual growth.

Our bodies are perfect machines. Left unhindered, they will fight off all disease, remove all toxins, and remain healthy. However, we are the ones that get in the way of our own health as we shall explain in this topic.

What Causes Disease?

In the last topic, we discussed how you have seven main

energy centres in your body, called chakras. Each chakra is responsible for sending certain frequencies of your life force energy to certain cells, organs, muscles and tissues around your body. One is healthy when their inner light is able to flow well to all the cells of the body. Remember, this light is electromagnetic and is used for many different biological processes. If sufficient light is unable to flow properly to any cells or organs, this will result in chronic health conditions.

It is well known from biological laboratory experiments that you can almost entirely repair a damaged cell in a single day just by illuminating the cell with light. This phenomenon is called photo-repair. What Professor Fritz-Albert Popp realised from his experiments was that a cancerous compound must cause cancer because it permanently blocks this light and scrambles it, so that photo-repair can't work anymore. Popp found that cancer patients had lost the coherence of light within them. In effect, their inner light was going out.

After further experimentation and research, Dr Reich (who discovered orgone energy) demonstrated that the orgone radiation was the same energy that the sun gave off. He was able to culture and inoculate what he called "SAPA Bions" of the cosmic orgone energy. When he placed live cancer cells next to the orgone "Bions," the cancer cells would die. Therefore, if we have sufficient orgone energy, or light energy, circulating around our bodies, we would be free of disease.

When something is acidic, this means it is an electron stealer, and if something is alkaline, this means it is an electron donor. Electron stealers take electrons away from electron donors, and so an area of high voltage always causes electrons to flow to an area of low voltage. As Dr Jerry Tennant discovered from his research, all disease occurs when your voltage is low, which means that your cells are in an electron stealer state. The higher the voltage in your cells, the greater the flow of the electromagnetic current around your body. By ensuring that our cells are electron donors (alkaline), we ensure we keep the voltage within us high. Without the ability to achieve at least a 7.88 pH, which is alkaline, and the necessary raw materials to make new cells, you cannot maintain your health, you cannot repair injuries, and you experience ageing and chronic disease as a result. When voltage drops to +30 mV (which occurs at the acidic pH of 6.48), cancer occurs. In his book Healing Is Voltage, Dr Jerry Tennant tells us, "You don't need drugs to heal. You need to make new cells that work to heal. To make good cells, you need voltage and a good diet. You also need to remove toxins from your body that damage cells and make you obese." Whenever the voltage drops, organs don't have enough horsepower to do their job, and they don't have the energy to get rid of toxic waste, so the toxins begin to accumulate. This is backed up by the research of Dr Otto Warburg, who was awarded the Nobel Prize in Physiology Or Medicine in 1931. He discovered that no disease, including cancer, can exist in an alkaline environment. Therefore, no disease can exist if the voltage of our cells is high.

What all this research shows is that disease occurs when our cells do not receive enough light energy, or orgone energy, or voltage. One simply needs to ensure they are getting enough life force energy to their cells in order to stay healthy. But how does one do this?

Diet

One of the main factors that impact the flow of light around the body is diet. In the last topic, we discussed that eating food is one of the main ways we replenish our inner light energy. When talking about diet, it is useful to talk in terms of light energy rather than calories - remember, we want to go beyond the illusory material reality of calories to the subtle reality of light energy. Different types of food have different concentrations of light particles, or photons, in them. Therefore, if we eat more foods that are rich in light energy, more energy can be used by our chakras. If we eat foods that are not rich in light energy, our chakras have less light energy to distribute around the body. Vegetables, fruits and nuts have very high concentrations of light particles (called biophotons) within them. Our cells are able to absorb this highly ordered frequency of light, allowing them to oscillate at a higher frequency. A higher frequency leads to a higher state of order and an enhanced style of cellular functioning. It is for this reason that Professor Popp considers the bio-photon content to be of far greater importance than just the nutrient or caloric content of a food.

Not only are vegetables, fruits and nuts rich in light, but, when digested, they are broken down into alkaline components that are distributed around the body. In contrast, meat, dairy products, eggs, most grains, coffee and alcohol are all broken down into acidic components when digested. To have a high voltage, the goal is not necessarily a perfect 100% of alkaline foods; it is recommended to have a diet of 80% alkaline and 20% acidic foods. In addition, unprocessed food contains voltage. Once we process food, most of the voltage seems to get released. We are designed to eat unprocessed food because they bring their own electrons. When you eat food that has been processed, your body must provide electrons from other sources to digest it.

Water is another big factor affecting the body's voltage. Our cells are 70% water. As the voltage of water is raised, more oxygen can be absorbed by the water. But if the voltage of water drops, oxygen leaves the water. Thus, as voltage begins to drop within us, oxygen leaves the cells. This has serious consequences. With a low voltage of water, this means our metabolism goes down, making it very difficult for cells to have enough energy to function. Furthermore, our bodies contain perhaps 1 trillion microorganisms. However, most of these are inactive as long as oxygen is present in the water of our bodies. But when oxygen levels drop because of a low voltage within the water, these bugs wake up. The first thing they want to do when they wake up is have you for lunch. If that wasn't bad enough, the toxins produced by these bugs can enter the bloodstream and cause infections and organ damage. As voltage continues to drop, it will go from electron donor to electron stealer status. Water from the ground contains electrons. We call this alkaline water. However, when we place chlorine and fluoride into the water, as what happens with our tap water, it turns into an electron stealer. Thus, every time we drink tap water, it steals electrons from us. In order to keep our voltage high, the water we drink must contain electrons and be free from toxins. You can buy water filters to remove fluoride, toxins and heavy metals from your drinking water. You can also put a slice of lemon, lime or orange into your glass of water – although these fruits contain acid, when they are fully digested, they are broken down into alkaline components.

If you ensure that your cells receive everything they need to function properly, your body will be able to heal itself from anything, and you will be in a great state of health. A cell is made up of a cell membrane and the inside is called a cytoplasm. The cell membrane is made of "good" fats. The cytoplasm is made of proteins. To be used, proteins and fats need vitamins and minerals. Therefore, in order for cells to have a high voltage, they need alkaline water, good fats, proteins, vitamins, minerals, oxygen, and light (from light-rich foods).

Many people have got it in their heads that in order to be spiritual, one must be vegetarian or vegan, but that simply isn't true. Feeling that you should or should not be doing something, or categorising certain diets as good and certain diets as bad, are all consequences of the mind. There is no one diet that is suitable for everyone, and there isn't a set diet for those who are spiritual. Everyone's bodies and vibrations are unique, and so we all have different requirements. One simply needs to listen to what their body is asking for; it is your body that you are feeding after all. If your body requires meat, eat some meat. It may not be appropriate to force a diet on yourself that your body simply isn't ready for. What you'll find is, as you raise your vibration, your body will automatically require more light rich foods, and it will be less attracted to dense foods like meat. This will be a natural switch. You will not need to force it upon yourself. Before my spiritual awakening, I used to eat only meat and some pasta or rice. I also drank a lot of alcohol and coffee. But now, the only foods I feel like eating are salads, soups, fruits and nuts. And the only things I drink are alkaline water and smoothies. But this isn't through forcing myself to eat and drink these things – my body just prefers these foods and drinks more now. However, if I tried to follow this diet before going through my spiritual awakening, I wouldn't have enjoyed it. I know you will go, or are already going, through the same experience as well.

But you must remember that being a vegetarian or vegan does not make you better or more spiritually advanced than others. If you think of yourself as a vegetarian or a vegan, you are still associating with ego labels. It is not about having a diet that your mind deems you should have, and it is not about doing what you think is cool, or trying to force a diet on yourself that you are not ready for. It is all about simply following what your body needs. Connect with your body and listen to it. Whatever food and drink it wants you to have, just have it. And whatever your body doesn't like or react well to, take those things away from your diet. It doesn't need to be more complicated than this. Many talk about wanting to be vegetarians or vegans because they don't want animals to be killed, but you must remember that all souls are eternal. The souls of animals never die. Only illusory material forms die. Therefore, you do not need to judge meat or any other food or drink as bad or wrong. Just continue with your spiritual progression, and you will naturally reduce your meat consumption without needing to force it upon yourself.

Another thing to consider is whether you are basing your diet on trying to achieve a certain body look. Everybody is different. A diet that helps one person achieve a certain look may not have the same effect on another person. But have you ever stopped and wondered why you want to look a certain way? The ego is telling you that you should look like this in order to be happy. And those thoughts are based on what you believe will make you more likeable, desirable, accepted, valued, and loved by others. The root of all this is believing that you are your body, rather than realising that the body is just a temporary tool that the real you is using. If you feel great and are in good health, why does it matter how you look? If your body is just a tool, and you are taking great care of that tool so that it is used in the most effective way possible, why does it matter how that tool looks? Focus on what diet helps you feel great, rather than what is going to help you get wash-board abs.

Let us also not confuse eating according to one's addictions as doing what the body wants. Addictions are things people use to regularly escape certain thoughts, feelings or emotions. Addictions are cravings of the mind, not the body. When one tunes into their body, they can decide in the moment what their body is asking for in order to ensure it has the right nutrients at all times. Impulse and spontaneous cravings are your body telling you it wants something. While addictions are predictable and repetitive patterns of behaviour; the opposite of spontaneous. What's more, body cravings are not triggered by anything that is external to you - the craving is spontaneous and comes from within. However, addictions are usually triggered by your mind's reaction to some sort of external situation. People also often choose food based on adverts or promotions that they see - again these are all outside influences, and are often not foods that your body actually wants. It is all about being in conscious control of your diet choices rather than being controlled by external influences.

Emotions

We have now established that if we have a diet that is alkaline and rich in light, vitamins, minerals, proteins and good fats, the chakras will have a good source of energy. However, although diet plays a major role in maintaining day-to-day health, one is unlikely to get seriously sick or develop a chronic health condition from dietary issues alone. We discussed in the last topic how suppressed emotions cause blockages in chakras, and blockages prevent light energy to flow from a chakra to its corresponding organs. A blockage in a chakra also prevents light energy rising up to be used by other chakras and other organs. Therefore, you could intake a great quantity of light by eating light-rich foods, breathing deeply and exposing your skin to sunlight, but if you have blockages in your chakras, all that light intake would almost be in vain. People often think that they are doing the right thing by holding in their emotions, but this leads to chakra blockages and, eventually, chronic health conditions. Yes, it may be appropriate to perhaps temporarily suppress certain emotions so that you do not have a negative effect on the others around you. But you must then, at the earliest possible chance, work on transforming these emotions as per the techniques already discussed in this course, otherwise, they will build up to become blockages in your chakras.

Dr Candace Pert, a neuropharmacologist who worked at Georgetown University Medical Centre, famously concluded from her scientific research that "Your body is your subconscious mind", and that our physical bodies can be changed by the emotions we experience. She explains how a feeling sparked in our mind will translate as a peptide being released somewhere. Organs, tissues, skin, muscles and endocrine glands all have peptide receptors on them and can access and store emotional information. This means the emotional memory is stored in many places in the body, not just (or even primarily) in the brain. Unexpressed emotions are literally lodged in the body. The unexpressed trauma of past experiences stored in the musculature and connective tissue of our bodies creates tension, blocks circulation, and can ultimately lead to pain and disease. She advised people to let all their emotions bubble to the surface, feel those emotions and understand them. In this way, one uses their consciousness to transform negative emotions into understanding, forgiveness and acceptance. Once integrated, the natural wisdom of the receptors will release interrupted healing, and restorative and regenerative processes can take over. By simply acknowledging emotions, they are expressed. In being expressed, emotions can then be transformed, even old emotions stored in body memory. She said, "Allowing emotions to surface into awareness and to be able to name one's emotions is the beginning of emotional exploration."

Dr Reich was able to apply his earlier research of psychological disorders to the behaviour of orgone. When energy is blocked by traumatic memories, and then stored in the tissues of the body, this can cause muscular tension. He termed this accumulation and blockage: "Armouring." This stagnate energy becomes "Deadly Orgone Energy." Dr Reich believed that Deadly Orgone Energy was largely responsible for psychological and mental disturbances in life forms, as well as the body's physical degeneration. He later discovered the therapeutic use of orgone's ability to clear these energetic blockages that exist within the body that would often be associated with major disease or illness, including cancer.

Emotions are the body's energetic responses to thoughts, and our thoughts are based on our beliefs. While being able to transform the low-vibrational emotions as they arise is an appropriate way to stay healthy, it is more efficient to drop all programmed beliefs, disassociate from the ego, and remember who you truly are. In so doing, you experience much fewer negative emotions, freeing up much more life force energy to be used by the body to keep itself in good health. For this reason, it is extremely rare to find a spiritually advanced person get sick unless their soul's chosen way of leaving their particular incarnation.

Stress

Stress is a vital factor in one's health. Whenever we feel any stress or fear, our sympathetic nervous system kicks in, which puts us in fight-or-flight mode. The sympathetic nervous system is the body's response to fear. The pupils dilate so we can see better, the heart rate and respiratory rate increase so we can run, fight or hide, more glucose is released into the bloodstream to make more energy available to our cells, and our blood flow is shunted to the extremities and away from our internal organs so we can move quickly if we need to. The immune system initially dials up and then dials down as adrenaline and cortisol flood the muscles, providing a rush of energy to either escape or fend off the stressor. Circulation moves out of our rational forebrain and is instead relayed to our hindbrain, so we have less capacity to think creatively and instead rely more on our instinct to instantly react. In the short term, all organisms can tolerate adverse conditions by fighting, hiding, or fleeing from an impending stressor. All of us are built for dealing with short-term bursts of stress. When the event is over, the body normally returns to balance. However, no organism in nature can endure living in emergency mode for extended periods of time. If we are consistently feeling stressed, not enough life force energy is able to be used for digestion, repair and the immune system.

Telomeres are the endcaps of the chromosomes in our cells, and they shorten slightly every time a cell divides. Telomerase is an enzyme that adds DNA molecules to the ends of telomeres. As we grow older, the chains of DNA in the telomeres on the ends of our chromosomes decline at a rate of about 1% a year. This makes telomere length an extremely stable marker of biological aging. When people are stressed, their cells die more quickly because of the wear and tear on their molecules. To replace the cells killed by stress, the body's cells have to divide more often to make replacements. As cells divide more frequently, their telomeres shorten more quickly. Stressed people lose telomere length fast, while healthy people have long telomeres. This explains why those who experience a lot of stress age more quickly than others, and why they seem to die at younger ages than those who know how to relax. You can see this clearly in the faces of US presidents - they always look considerably older at the end of their term compared to when they took office, and this is because of the incredible amounts of stress they regularly need to endure as part of their job.

Exercise

We all know exercise is good for us, but how does it relate to our body's voltage? Well, if you take a quartz crystal and squeeze it with a pair of pliers, it will emit electrons. This is called the piezoelectric effect. Our muscles are piezoelectric crystals. So when we exercise, our muscles create electrons. The muscles are also rechargeable batteries, so the movement of our muscles not only gives us electrons, but it also re-charges our muscle batteries. Exercise is a major way the body acquires electrons and improves its voltage. What's more, exercise helps us release tension and allows us to feel relaxed afterwards. As a result of being less mentally and emotionally stressed and more relaxed, more life force energy is able to flow around the body. Relaxing exercises such as Tai Chi and Qigong are specifically designed to help the flow of light, or chi, around the body.

Responding To Health Conditions

All sickness, ailments and health conditions actually ought not be seen as bad or negative things. They are a way for your true self to tell you that you need to take certain actions, whether that be releasing suppressed emotions, relieving your stress by taking a break and relaxing for a while, or perhaps to change your diet or lifestyle. This is not the first way your true self tries to communicate to you - your true self will always try to guide you in gentler ways first, but if you do not listen to the subtle guidance within you then your true self allows you to experience a health condition as you will more likely listen to their guidance that way. But your true self does not cause your illness - you have caused it in some way (as previously discussed), and your true self has tried to guide you to take actions to rectify the cause before it turns into a health condition. That's why those who live from their heart and always follow their inner guidance never get sick. But if you do not listen to your true self's guidance, perhaps by continuing to resist suppressed emotions that are trying to come to the surface, or continuing with your stressful lifestyle when you need a break, your true self has no other choice but to allow you to get sick so that you can finally get the hint.

The fear of death is by far the biggest fear that people have, and this is why we react so negatively to sickness and health conditions. But our fear of death is so hidden in our subconscious that it negatively affects how we live our lives without us even knowing about it. By getting sick or ill, this fear is able to rise to the surface so you can deal with it. Once you make peace with your inevitable death, you are able to completely relax your being. This can be so clearly seen in patients who are told they have a terminal illness- they are forced to come to terms with their death. Once they do, they begin to relax and enjoy life by doing the things they've always wanted to do. But you do not need to get sick to come to terms with your own death; you can do it right here, right now if you so wish. By doing this, you can completely relax and live without fear, which would allow you to enjoy life. When relaxed, fearless and enjoying life, light will be flowing properly around your body, keeping you healthy. This is why spiritually advanced people, who have already experienced the death of their ego (i.e. they've become aware of who they really are) will never get sick, unless their soul is choosing to leave that particular incarnation.

Why do you think cancer returns in some patients? And why is it that when some people manage to treat their health condition, they experience a different condition soon after? It is because these patients have not dealt with the underlying cause of their health conditions. Health conditions are catalysts for our spiritual progression as they can push us to evaluate our lives, re-establish priorities, and achieve emotional or spiritual breakthroughs. When this happens, one can be healed instantly. However, if someone does not use their health condition to achieve any breakthroughs or learn any lessons, they will rarely be healed in the long-term, or, if they are healed, they will experience another catalyst, perhaps in the form of a different health condition. At best, modern medicine can only put a band aid on chronic health conditions. At worst, they can do more harm than good. The real healing occurs within.

Genes

Many people believe that their health conditions are caused by their genes, but only 2% of disorders are actually due to single gene defects. Therefore, the great majority of us are not at the mercy of our genes - we are in control of our own health.

Topic 17 Exercises

Day 1

At the end of the day today, I would like you to make a note of what you ate, and roughly estimate what percentage of the foods were alkaline and what percentage were acidic. Are you surprised by the result?

Day 2

For today's exercise, just notice what you eat and why you are eating those particular foods. What is your decision to have those foods based on? Is it a routine? Is it from addictions? Is it from some kind of outside influence? Or did you listen to what your body actually needs? Notice how your body feels after each meal. Are you still hungry? We often still feel hungry after meals because we did not give the body the nutrients it was asking for.

Day 3

Today, we are going to base all our food decisions on what our body wants in the moment. You are not going to pre-plan anything and you are not going to let anything or anyone influence your food decisions. When it is time to eat, close your eyes, detach from your thoughts, and ask your body what it needs. Wait until you get the body's answer. How did this affect your decisions on what to eat? How did you feel after each meal when you did this? Did you feel different compared to how you felt after yesterday's meals?

Day 4

I'd like you to do a Qigong or Tai Chi exercise session today. You can find many on Youtube. If you don't know where to start, on the 'High Vibe Livin' Youtube channel there is a playlist of all my favourite sessions.

Day 5

We are going to focus on stress today. Make a list of the three things that you are consistently most stressed about. This may be your job, your relationships, or anything else that isn't short-terms. As we learned in this topic, stress is extremely harmful to your health. So, with each thing you listed, I want you to think of ways where you can eradicate this stress from your life. Is there some action you could take? Is there a conversation you could have with someone? Is there a different attitude you could have? If you haven't been able to identify anything that you could do to help reduce your stress, it may be time to really think about whether having this stress in your life is worth the harmful effects. If not, then you may need to cut those things out of your life for your own benefit.

Day 6

At the end of your day today, I want you to really come to terms with the fact that your body will one day die. This may be scary at first, but as we learned in this topic, it is essential if you want to enjoy life. Notice what emotions or feelings arise as you try to come to terms with your death. Allow those feelings to come to the surface, and feel them fully until they are transformed. Then remind yourself that the real you is eternal, and only the illusory you can die.

Day 7

Today, I simply want you to notice the connection between your mind and body. Whenever you catch yourself experiencing any emotional or mental stress, tune in to how this stress is affecting your body. How do you feel as a result of this stress? And anytime you experience positive thoughts or emotions, tune in to how your body feels. Do you feel how your thoughts and emotions affect your body as a result of this exercise?

TOPIC 18 - MEDITATION

We have so far talked in this course about the illusory perception we have of this world. This mainly comes from associating ourselves with our ego, our false self. We have also explained how the spiritual journey is a journey of self-discovery, where we dissolve all illusions to discover our true divine nature. In my experience, this would be almost impossible without meditation.

What is Meditation?

Meditation is all about taking the time to explore and understand yourself. This is the primary aim of meditation. There is no wrong way to meditate as long as this primary aim is fulfilled. You can sit down, lie down, stand up, or even walk. You can have your eyes closed or open. You can be still or you can be doing some activity. To explore and understand your true self, you must disassociate from your ego in some way. As we go about our day, we are so easily distracted by our ego's constant thoughts. When we are distracted by thoughts, we are unable to really explore and understand our true selves. Therefore, we must make time to detach from the ego in order to grow spiritually, and this is what meditation is all about.

There are many different ways one can disassociate from

their ego. For instance, one can do an activity that they really enjoy. When enjoying an activity, you are likely to be completely present. Your ego cannot exist when you are present; it only lives in the past and future. Or perhaps you could do something that brings out your creative side. Your ego is not creative - it simply uses what it has experienced in the past in order to create. But when you are creating something unique and different, particularly when you create it without really thinking about it, you are allowing the Divine within you to come out and play, and your ego becomes dormant. Perhaps you may lose yourself in music or dance - this self that is being lost is your false self, your ego. Maybe you like to spend time out in nature and get lost in the beauty of it all. Maybe you like to have loving sex with your partner, where you lose yourself in them. Perhaps you find it easy to focus on your breath or bodily sensations or a candle for a prolonged period of time. All of these are examples of different types of meditation as they all involve you disassociating from your ego by taking your attention away from your ego's thoughts and completely focusing on something else.

However, most people are either unable to easily do these types of activities regularly, or these types of activities are not suitable for them for whatever reason. The best types of meditation for such people therefore involve becoming aware of the ego. In order to do this, one must be in a state of stillness and silence. When still and silent, you are able to easily become aware of the constant flows of energies of the ego's thoughts and connected emotions. When you are busy, not only are you less able to notice your ego's thoughts and emotions, but you are more easily swept up by them. Your ego uses the energy of your mind and body to continuously generate energies within you, but your awareness, your true self, is always still and silent. There-fore, when you consciously choose to be still and silent, you are better able to remember who you really are and observe the ego for what it really is; an illusion. Therefore, you have two main ways of disassociating from your ego during meditation; you can either shift your focus com-pletely away from your ego's thoughts and onto some-thing else, or you can become aware of your ego. Only awareness can be aware of the ego as the ego cannot be aware of itself. So when you are aware of your ego, you are being your true self and are detaching from your false self. You will find that when your bring your awareness to your ego, your ego no longer exists. It can only exist in your subconscious mind when you are not aware of it.

There are a great many ways to meditate. I encourage you try different methods until you find one that suits you. Osho's The Book of Secrets contains 112 tried and tested methods, so this is a good place to start. When meditat-ing for the first few times, it will be extremely hard to not get distracted by your ego. You have been associating yourself with the voice in your head all your life, which has been talking to you continuously for many years, and so you cannot expect to be able to switch all that off the first time you try. It may even be shocking at first when you realise how loud and out-of-control the voice in your head really is. However, do not be too hard on yourself, and do not worry if you don't feel your meditation has been successful the first time you try. Having the will to go beyond your ego is the first step. The more you prac-tice, the more it will get easier, I guarantee you that. Just try out different methods until you find one that suits you. When giving a method a try, try it a few times before deciding whether it is appropriate for you or not. You will find that the better you are at disassociating from your ego, the happier and more relaxed you will be. Eventually, life can become one big long meditation, at which point you have reached the enlightened state of permanent peace, love, happiness and joy.

Conscious Breathing

Of course, may of us lead quite busy lives, and while we may find it easier to detach from our ego when we make time during meditations, it is often difficult to disassociate from our egos when engaging with life and other people. One quick and effective tool you can use is to take deep, slow conscious breaths. Most people spend their life unconsciously taking fast, shallow breaths because they are completely engaged with their ego's thoughts most of the time, and these egoic thoughts keep them in a constant state of fear and stress. When you are stressed or mentally engaged with something, you take short, fast, shallow breaths. In fact, if you don't take charge of your breathing, you will take fast, shallow breaths by default. Have you ever noticed when someone is scrolling through their phone, watching TV or are on their computer, and they suddenly turn their attention away from their electronics, they do a huge inhale through their nose? This is because when we are glued to our electronics, we become zombie-like. We're hardly breathing. We are in a trance. The same occurs when we are associating with the ego – our breathing becomes unconscious because we are focusing on our thoughts, and we become like zombies as a result. To snap yourself out of the trance, you must consciously take charge of your breathing, and take deep, slow breaths. By bringing your conscious attention to your breathing, you take the attention off your thoughts, and you return to the present moment. And remember, only our true selves live in the present, so when you focus only on your breathing, rather than focusing on the ego's thoughts which direct your attention to the past or future, you become your true self. You will notice that it is impossible to feel fear, anger, guilt or any other low-vibrational emotion when you take long, slow, deep breaths.

The ego is associated with the most primitive part of the brain, called the amygdala. This is responsible for our automatic fight-or-flight responses. These responses are often irrational and unconscious. It is the most primitive part of the brain and is often called the 'emotional brain'. When used, it creates fear within the body by triggering the secretion of adrenaline, and increasing the heart rate, blood pressure and breathing. However, our neocortex is our rational brain, or wise brain, or 'higher brain'. When used, it can stop you from acting impulsively and emotionally, and helps you think and act rationally. When you are using the amygdala, your breathing is fast and shallow. However, when you take slow, deep breaths, this switches off the amygdala and activates the neocortex. Slow, deep breathing also allows you to use your prefrontal cortex, which helps regulate emotions. This is why people are advised to take deep breaths when they are angry or stressed. By slowing down and deepening your breathing, you are effectively switching off your ego.

With conscious breathing, your level of consciousness changes. Conscious breathing relaxes you, and helps you feel peaceful, more joyful, more at one with everything, more energetic, and more full of love. If you don't believe that your breathing can make such a dramatic difference,

I encourage you to close your eyes for one minute, take long, slow, deep breaths, and pause for three seconds between the inhale and exhale. It may help to hold in the breath during those three seconds. Notice how you feel during those three seconds. Pure bliss and peace, and this is just one of many, many breathing techniques you can do.

Conscious breathing is extremely good for your health as well. If you remember from previous topics, we discussed how one of the ways we replenish our life force energy is through our breathing. But when we take fast, shallow breaths, we do not intake as much life force energy from the zero point field as we do when taking slow, deep breaths. And when there is less life force energy flowing through our bodies, our health can deteriorate. Through deep conscious breathing, we ensure we intake more life force energy, which means more light can be distributed around our bodies. And as we have learned in the previous two topics, the more life force energy that can be distributed around our bodies, the healthier we are. To be efficient with one's breathing and consistently take in a lot of light with each breath, one must breathe into their belly, not their lungs. When you see a young child breathe, their belly goes up and down. But as we get older, we become stressed, and we no longer breathe into the belly. Let's try an exercise now - take as big a breath as possible but only by moving your lungs, not your belly. When you think you have reached capacity, now try and take more breath by breathing into your belly. You will find that you are able to take slightly more if you use the belly. Not only do deep breaths bring the body more life force energy, but, as we know, it brings oxygen as well. Deep breaths are more efficient - they allow your body to fully exchange incoming oxygen with outgoing carbon dioxide. By taking deep breaths, arterial oxygenation improves, and more oxygen enters our blood stream. The more oxygen that can be given to our cells, the higher our metabolism, and the higher the voltage within our body. As we learned in the previous topic, this leads to better health. I bet you didn't know there were so many different dimensions to breathing!

Brainwaves

There are five basic brainwaves that are picked up by a modern EEG. They are Delta, Theta, Alpha, Beta and Gamma waves. Each type of wave has a different frequency. Each type of brainwave is an indication of the type of activity the brain is engaged in. For instance, Beta is the signature brain wave of people with anxiety, people experiencing frustration, and people under stress. Negative emotions such as anger, fear, blame, guilt, and shame produce large flares of Beta. Beta is required for processing information and for linear thinking, but it inhibits many beneficial cellular functions, and your body ages much faster when your brainwaves are at a Beta frequency. Beta is clearly then the brainwave associated with the ego.

Gamma is the highest recorded brainwave frequency, and is most prevalent at times when the brain is learning, making associations between phenomena, and integrating information from many different parts of the brain. A brain producing lots of gamma waves reflects complex neural organisation and heightened awareness. When monks were asked to meditate on compassion, large flares of gamma were found in their brains. The monks reported entering a state of bliss. Gamma is associated with very high levels of intellectual function, creativity, integration, peak states, and being present. Gamma waves also help the immune system, the growth and repair of cells, and helps regulate stress hormones like cortisol. Clearly, when the brain is producing Gamma waves, it is an indication that the person is aligning with their true self.

Therefore, when we think in terms of frequency, the ideal brainwave state to aim for is Gamma. This brainwave state can more easily be achieved during meditation. The frequency of Gamma waves are between 40 and 100 Hz. You can find sounds with such frequencies on Youtube. As we have learned, because of the physics principle of entrainment, when you surround yourself with high frequencies, this encourages your vibration to rise in order to match those higher frequencies. Therefore, listening to Gamma wave sounds is a good way to encourage your brain to be in the Gamma brainwave state.

Is There A Shortcut?

Often people look for shortcuts during their spiritual awakening journeys; they don't want to do the daily meditations, the daily struggles against the false self, the self-reflection, the transforming of suppressed emotions, the self-improvement. But I'm afraid there is no shortcut. It is tough work but it's absolutely worth it. You chose to come here on this Earth at this time because you believed you could do this tough work. And I believe you can do it too. How boring would life be without challenges anyway? So you can either continue the life you are living now, or you can do some work on yourself for a relatively short period of time until you are eventually living heaven on earth. The more spiritual work you do, the happier, healthier, and more fulfilled you will be.

There are man, many ways to meditate. However, I have purposely chosen not to encourage any one specific type of technique in this topic. Different meditations work for different people, and you will find that different types of meditations work for you at different stages of your spiritual journey. I encourage you to research and try out different techniques to find what works best for you. You might even make up some new techniques of your own. Remember, what you are looking for are techniques that help you disassociate from your ego in some way. The following daily exercises are just suggestions, but if you want to ignore them and do your own meditations instead, then please do.

Topic 18 Exercises

<u>Day 1</u>

In today's meditation, close your eyes and simply focus on your breathing. Don't let a breath go by without being fully conscious of it. This means being present with all aspects of the breath - this includes the exhale, not just the inhale. Take long, slow, deep breaths, and notice how this conscious breathing makes you feel. If you catch yourself being distracted by thoughts, immediately just bring your attention back to your breath. Do this exercise for at least 10 minutes.

<u>Day 2</u>

In today's meditation, light some incense or a scented candle, or have anything that smells good nearby. Close your eyes and inhale the smell. Get to know the smell. Feel as if a connection is being made between you and the object giving off the smell. Feel as if this object is trying to please you with its smell. Now realise this object is you. You are pleasing yourself. How wonderful.

Day 3

In today's meditation, take deep, slow, conscious breaths. As you inhale, visualise yourself drawing down light, which enters your crown chakra and works its way down to the root chakra. Feel the light reaching each chakra. On the exhale, feel and visualise this light spreading out from your chakras to all the cells of your body. Do this exercise for 15 minutes.

Day 4

Identify an activity to do today. This activity must be something that you can lose yourself in, something that keeps you in the present moment throughout. This could be any activity at all. Make some time to do this activity today.

Day 5

Go on to Youtube and find a Gamma frequency video. Play this video through earphones while you meditate. Clear your mind and notice how these frequencies make you feel. Tune in to your body throughout.

Day 6

Take 10 minutes out of your day today to pick a plant, or tree, or a patch of grass that you like. Now sit by it and feel at one with it. Lose yourself in it. Inspect it, get to know it, appreciate its beauty. Ensure you detach from the voice in your head as you do this. Put all your attention on this object. How do you feel as you do this exercise?

Day 7

We will try shutting off the sensory input to our body today. So sit or lie down inside in silence and stillness. Wear an eye mask over your eyes, and put noise-cancelling earphones in your ears. When you shut off the senses, the ego does not have the input it usually uses to create thoughts. It may start to visualise something or replay a memory – make sure it doesn't distract you with this. Enjoy this inner silence and stillness.

TOPIC 19 - THE ASCENSION JOURNEY

The intention behind sharing all the information in this course is to help you raise your vibration and level of consciousness by guiding you through your spiritual awakening. In this topic, I will talk about common things that people experience on their spiritual awakening journeys. This information will help explain many of the inner feelings and changes you experience as you spiritually progress.

Raising Your Vibration

Progressing on your spiritual journey is the most satisfying and fulfilling thing you could do in life. However, you cannot expect to develop spiritually and keep everything about your old life. It helps to think about this in terms of vibration – your old life was based around a lower vibration; this includes the vibration of the food you ate, the activities you engaged in, perhaps your job, your friends, where you lived, your thoughts and emotions. As you raise your inner vibration, many aspects of your old life will no longer feel right anymore. You will be able to feel how these aspects of your old life drag your vibration down, and so you will feel the need to release or change those things.

For instance, you may start to be a lot less interested in, or no longer enjoy, the activities you used to partake in. For me, this meant no longer watching the news, or listening to the music I used to listen to, or going to bars and clubs, and I even stopped my participation competitive football which I used to love. I felt how all these things were keeping me in a lower vibration, so stopping them made me feel a lot more relaxed. Instead, you may find yourself becoming interested in new activities that match your higher vibration or even help you raise your vibration. For me, this included meditation, qigong, sun gazing, looking at the stars, being out in nature, and dancing. I encourage you to notice your vibration and how you feel when doing all your activities, cut out the things pulling you down, and try new activities that your heart is guiding you towards.

What's more, you are likely to find that you no longer feel comfortable around many of your friends and even family members. As you awaken, you become more aware of the negative influences the people around you have on you, and you become aware of how your vibration now lowers when you around those people that you used to spend so much time around before. It is important not to fight this feeling and not to force the continuation of those relationships that no longer resonate. This will only cause you much distress. Even though your friends and family may initially react angrily to you wanting to now distance yourself from them, you are just doing what feels right for you. Do you really want to sacrifice your spiritual awakening just to satisfy those around you? You do not need to look upon these changes as bad - it is just a consequence of you raising your vibration. Letting those friends and family members go does not mean you no longer love them; it is about wishing them well on their journey and ensuring you are able to continue with yours. You can still love people from a distance. Your friends and family may also argue that you are being selfish by following your inner guidance, but I assure you this is not the case. We are all on different paths, and if someone truly loves you, they will allow you the freedom to pursue your path without judging you or wanting to change or control you. If someone gets angry at you for doing what's best for you, then it is just a sign that their love is conditional - the condition being that you have a close relationship with them. You will find that you do end up letting go of many people in your life, but you are being guided to do this intentionally. Once you have made the conscious decision to spiritually awaken, your true self guides you to the actions that will best help you progress on your spiritual journey. Often, without the distraction of other people, one can turn inward and explore who they truly are, which can only be good for one's spiritual progression. What's more, if most of the people around you are of a lower vibration, then it is best to escape that environment so that you have nothing energetically holding you back from continuing with your spiritual progress. However, this does not mean that you will never be close to those people again - they, too, may spiritually awaken at a later date, and you may find yourselves reconnecting again once your vibrations are more closely matched.

Another common occurrence among those who spiritually awaken is that they no longer enjoy their current job.

Again, they may become aware of the negative influences their job has on them. For instance, they may become aware that they are often stressed while working, or they may find that they experience a lot of low-vibrational emotions while at work, or they may simply lose all interest in what they do. Each job, workplace, colleague, and building all have their own vibration. If your vibration used to be a match for your job role, but then you raised your vibration, naturally your job role will no longer feel right. If something doesn't feel right, act upon it. For your own good, it is best not to try forcing yourself to stay in your old role out of fear of the future – this is just postponing the inevitable and will actually lower your vibration. Remember, you will always have what you need, so what is there to be scared of? You will be guided towards something else that matches your higher vibration – this may come in the form of new opportunities that suddenly come your way, or it may come from divine inspiration to start your own business.

There are many other things about your life that you will naturally feel like changing as you raise your vibration. Remember, everything has a vibration. This includes cities and neighbourhoods, so as you raise your vibration, you may feel the need to move to a different area. Different types of music, books and TV shows all have different vibrations as well, so the genres you are interested in may change. I no longer watch certain programs I used to like because I realised how depressing they were. You will likely also find that your diet naturally changes. As you raise your vibration, you will find that you crave less of the denser foods and drinks, like meats, alcohol, complex carbohydrates, and coffee, and you will want to eat more vegetables, fruits and nuts, and drink clean water.

You may also find that your appetite gradually reduces. This is because your new diet will contain so much light, that your body will not need as much food in order to get the light it needs. As you raise your vibration, you become more aware of the vibrations of everything, and you start to consciously choose what kind of vibrations you want to surround yourself with. Whenever you feel you want to change something about your life, no matter how big the decision is, do not panic. In fact, see it as evidence and a reflection of your own internal change. My advice is to go with the flow and see where it takes you.

Changing Beliefs & Perception

On your spiritual journey, your beliefs are likely to change drastically. Your old third-dimensional life was based on negative, limiting beliefs based on the illusions of materiality and separation. As you progress, your beliefs will change to be more in line with the truth of oneness and unconditional love. Beliefs are the lens through which you see life, so as your beliefs change, your perception of the world will change. Even if your external reality does not change much, your life will appear completely different because the lens through which you perceive it will have changed. However, your beliefs generate your thoughts, your thoughts trigger emotions, and your thoughts and emotions are what shape the type of reality you experience. Therefore, changes to your beliefs will eventually manifest as changes in your external reality. Remember, your external reality is simply a mirror to your internal reality. Before my awakening, I used to be consumed with thoughts and emotions of fear, anger and separation, and I did not see much beauty and joy in life. But now I am much more at peace and full of love and joy. As a result of this inner change, I started really noticing the sounds of birds, the stars, the clouds, and all the colours and smells of nature. All these things were there before, but I just wasn't focused on them. I have also manifested great things in my life by getting rid of my limiting beliefs and using my powers of creation. And I have no doubt that you will have similar experiences as your beliefs change.

Body Changes

Our graduation to fourth density is unique. It is unique because we are taking our bodies with us. Normally, during graduation to fourth density, our third density bodies would need to die so that we could reincarnate into a fourth density body. However, for the first time ever in our galaxy, our bodies are being converted to fourth density bodies while we are alive, and we will continue living in these same bodies as we transition to fourth density. Those who have made the conscious choice to spiritually awaken are likely to make the graduation, and so they will be the ones that experience the changes in their bodies. As these changes occur, you may notice certain "ascension symptoms", as they are sometimes called. These symptoms include extreme tiredness, blurry vision, disturbances in sleep patterns, third eye and heart chakra pressure, very vivid dreams, ringing in the ears, and wanting to drink a lot more water. It is important to take care of yourself as these changes occur. If you feel like you need to take it easy then take it easy. If you feel like drinking more water or eating more food, then just go with the flow. If you do experience disturbances in your sleeping pattern, don't judge it as a bad thing, just adapt to it.

Heart Guidance

The information you consume has a huge influence on your beliefs and therefore your life, so it is very important to only take what resonates with you. Whether it be from this course, online research, other books, the news, anything; please use your heart and intuition to guide you as to what is your truth. If part of this course resonates with you but other parts don't, please ignore the parts that don't resonate with you. If things you read or watch online or on the TV don't resonate, then please don't accept them as fact. If parts of a religion's texts resonate but other parts don't, then please don't feel that you have to take the whole religion as your truth. Your heart and intuition are your best guides because they are how your true self communicates to you. No matter how adamant or forceful people are with their opinions, perspectives and "facts", always use your inner guidance system to determine your own personal truth. In this way, you become your own priest, guru, rabbi, or imam. You have an inner guide that is far more spiritually advanced than any other human. Align with this guide and there is no need to have any other guide. The spiritual journey is a personal journey within. The journey is best undertaken with as little outside influence as possible. While resources like this course can give you a good start as to what kind of things you could explore, and can point you in certain directions based on other people's experiences, ultimately, you are the one who makes the decisions for your life. You are the one in charge of creating your reality. This is your journey, not anyone else's, and your journey is unique. If you rely on someone to tell you what to do and what not to do, you have given your power away and are not really experiencing true spirituality.

Focusing On Yourself First

World events are distractions from your internal environment, but the kingdom of heaven is within you now. Luckily, you can only consciously focus on one thing at a time, so will you choose to consciously focus on the external distractions and the ego's thoughts on those distractions, or will you choose to focus on heaven within you? This doesn't mean one should ignore everything around them, but at this stage of your spiritual awakening, it is important to turn your focus inward so you can remember who you really are. It is the most important thing. The biggest change you can make to this world is to raise your own vibration. When enough people raise their vibration, the world will change automatically to reflect this. When you have transformed within, you will be in the appropriate place to start helping others raise their vibration. If you have not discovered who you truly are, your ego will be involved in any help you try to give. When you remember, and align with, your true self, then you can truly help others from the state of unconditional love. This is because you will have realised that all is one. It is like how a parent should put on their oxygen mask before helping their child put on theirs - it is almost useless to try to help others if you haven't fully helped yourself first. When you are ready, the opportunities to help others will come to you.

The Difference Between Awakening, Ascension, Enlightenment & Graduation

What is a spiritual awakening? A spiritual awakening can be described as the start of the journey of peeling away the layers of illusions created by the mind. A spiritual awakening is about starting to wake up from the dream of separation. A spiritual awakening occurs when an inner spark of curiosity is triggered within you. This spark encourages you to question your reality and explore the realms of the unknown. The awakening is the process of shaking yourself out of the trance your ego put you in, and starting to become more conscious.

Ascension is about raising your level of consciousness, your inner vibration, from the third-dimensional frequency band of materiality and separation, to higher-dimensional frequency bands. Once you have spiritually awakened, you literally start ascending in frequency. The fifth-dimensional state of consciousness is what has been described as heaven - it is not a place but a state of consciousness that can be achieved right now if you so choose. All humans on Earth now are being encouraged to ascend to at least the fourth dimension as it is now time for our collective graduation to the next level of experience of reality. Those who do not sufficiently ascend in frequency by the time the graduation process has finished will not make the graduation to the new Earth, and will need to reincarnate elsewhere until they are ready to graduate.

Enlightenment is the permanent state of pure bliss, peace, unconditional love, joy and oneness. This state is discovered once a person has dissolved all illusions within their mind and has come to fully remember who they truly are. This is done by the gradual process of activating and balancing all one's chakras. Enlightenment describes the state one is in when they have fully ascended to the highest possible frequency. But you do not need to be enlightened in order to ascend to make the graduation to fourth density.

Graduation is the term I have used in this course to describe the process of Earth's and humanity's transition to fourth density. You can think of the density as the vibration of our planet, bodies and surroundings. To graduate, one needs to have a level of consciousness of at least the fourth dimension, and so must have fully activated their heart chakra. More information on the requirements for graduation can be found in the next levels of the course, but as long as you follow the guidance within this first level of the course, as well as your inner guidance, you will make the graduation.

You will find on your journey that you will drift in and out of association with your ego, but as you progress, more of your day will be experienced through the eyes of the Divine within you without the filters of your ego. It may sometimes feel you are going backwards on your spiritual journey, or that the ego is gaining more power over you, but, my friend, once you have started your spiritual journey, it is only a forward path. Once you have seen how a magic trick has created an illusion, you cannot be fooled by it anymore. Different experiences and challenges can help you become aware of different sides of the ego, but it has not gained anything new since you started your spiritual awakening. You may just become more aware of the ego. Its hold over your thoughts and emotions are becoming more obvious but not stronger. A fly can be on your skin for a long time and you may not consciously notice it, but if someone points it out to you, you can't stop noticing it. The only thing that changes is your awareness of it. You can only swat away the fly once you become aware of it. The ego is just like that fly – you can swat it away only when you become aware of it. The same fly may return to your skin, but you are now aware of it and can more easily swat it away in the future. Similarly, your ego may try to distract you, but because you are more aware of it, it is less able to distract you and you can deal with it easily.

The Key to 5D

This course is called *The Key to 5D* as it aims to guide you to ascend to the fifth-dimensional state of consciousness, known as heaven. The 'key' to this 5D realm is **True Unconditional Love**. As we have repeatedly discussed, true love is the recognition of your divine oneness with something or someone. By truly loving someone or something, you have realised your divinity, you have seen their divinity, and you have recognised your oneness with them. By experiencing true love, or oneness, or truth, you will unlock the gate to heaven. True love *is* the secret key to 5D.

Topic 19 Exercises

Day 1

Your ego only operates when you are on autopilot; in this state, you are not putting your full awareness onto the present moment. So, as you do anything today, bring your full awareness to it. If you are cooking, become fully aware of all the ingredients, the smells, the way you are cooking. If you are walking, be fully aware of your surroundings, your body, the temperature, the wind. When on the train, become fully aware of your surroundings, how your body is feeling, and your breath. Even when you are using the toilet, bring your full awareness to the present moment. Anywhere you are, anything you do, bring awareness to it. Don't do anything on autopilot.

Day 2

Today is all about feeling how your vibration is affected by the vibrations around you. Do you feel that the people you interact with are pulling you down or up? Is your job pulling your vibration down or up? Are the activities you do increasing your vibration or lowering it? What were the times your vibration was at its highest today, and when was it at its lowest?

Day 3

Today, take some time to think about the people, activities, and things in your life that you feel are no longer matching your vibration. Are there family members or friends who you feel are always having a negative influence on your vibe? What about the place you live – does it feel too dense now? Is your body crying out for a change in diet? Does your job not feel right anymore? Are certain TV programmes negatively affecting your vibration? Does a lot of the music you used to listen to now put you in a lower-vibrational state?

Day 4

For all those things identified in the previous exercise, start to take actions to remedy the situation. If the people around you are having a negative effect on your vibration, it is time to let them go. If the area you reside in feels too dense, use your heart to guide you as to where to move to. What type of foods is your body crying out for? If there are activities that no longer match your vibration, look to cut them out. Follow your guidance in trying new activities that may increase your vibration. If your job is pulling you down, use intuition to guide you as to what your next career move could be.

Day 5

Go about your day today with total love. Feel your oneness with your surroundings. Feel your oneness with everyone around you. You should be getting better at feeling oneness by now. Doesn't it feel great every time you remember the oneness of creation? Every day can be like this. What is there to be angry about? What is there to fear? You are the universe. You are eternal and infinite. With this knowledge, what other state could you be in than love?

Day 6

Go about your day today as usual. There is no particular exercise to do today. Notice any differences in how you now go about your day compared to how you went about your days before starting this course? Are you more aware of your things? Are you better able to detach from the voice in your head? Do you have a more positive perspective and outlook on life? Are you happier? Do you feel more at peace? What a miraculous transformation you have made in such a short period of time. I am so proud of you!

Day 7

We have tried a few different meditations in this course. I'm sure you have tried some other ones on your spiritual awakening journey as well. For the last exercise of this level of the course, just enjoy your favourite meditation.

AFTERWORD

Congratulations on finishing this first level of the course. I hope it has been some help in guiding you along the miraculous transformation you are now experiencing. However, the spiritual journey does not stop here. Continue to follow your inner guidance, which is your heart and intuition, to keep learning more truth and raise your vibration. If you feel so guided, levels 2 and 3 of the course are available for you to buy on Amazon or through my website.

What's more, just know that you are never alone on your journey as I am always here if you ever need me. If you would like a spiritual support session or healing session with me, or if you'd like to come to one of our spiritual retreats, then you can book through my website: www.highvibelivin.co.uk.

I love you and I am so honoured you have allowed me to help you on your journey. I wish you all the best for the remainder of your ascension.

Printed in Great Britain
by Amazon